The Rhymer

and

Other Helps for Poets

Revised and Enlarged

by
Nel Modglin

DORRANCE & COMPANY • *Philadelphia and Ardmore, Pa.*

ACKNOWLEDGMENTS

Permission was granted by the following authors and poets whose work appears in this book: Jim Arpy, Monica Boyce, Marjorie Culver, Magny Landstad Jensen, Thelma Scott Kiser, and Isabel H. Lancaster, to whom I offer my sincere gratitude.

For her help in correcting this manuscript, I also express thanks to my sister, LaVerne Brainard.

Copyright © 1977 by Nel Modglin
All Rights Reserved
ISBN 0-8059-2421-3
Printed in the United States of America

For
SHERIDAN Y. MAYNARD
(1905-1959)

*In memory
of our years as
husband and wife*

Contents

Foreword	vii
PART I—*The Rhymer*	3
PART II—*Helps for the Poet*	
Glossary of Poetic Terms	115
Six Modern Poetry Forms	125
What Is Meter?	131
Giving Your Poem a Title	132
Oriental Poetry Forms	133
Bring Me My Bow of Burning Gold	136
Index to the Rhymer	141

The creative person knows the heights of exhilaration and the deepest valleys of despair. His greatest curse is awareness that he will never achieve perfection, though if that were somehow possible, he would never recognize or concede it.
—Jim Arpy

Foreword

Poietes (Greek)—one who makes

A poet is a maker whose most important needs are words and the ability to use them correctly. Words are symbols, a way of showing others what one sees, hears, smells, tastes, touches, and thinks.

Most of all, a poet must have desire and dedication. These are two of the channels through which inspiration comes.

Samuel Johnson has said that rhyming is "joining music with reason."

When learning to write rhymed poetry, remember that the rhyme is based on the accented vowel of the syllable and the consonants must be different, as in an-noy, de-ploy. Therefore, words in this book are listed according to phonetic sound: none, nun, listed under UN. Note: excess and obsess are not rhymes. Although the consonants *c* and *s* are different, they have the same sound.

Words that are often pronounced two ways, as OO/U, are marked with an asterisk at the head of the column. Foreign words that are in common use, and a few near rhymes, have been included. All words are listed alphabetically, under the number of syllables that they contain.

Part I
THE RHYMER

A

ay
aye
bay
bey
brae
bray
chay
chez
clay
day
dey
dray
fay
feh
fey
flay
fray
gay
gray
hay
hey
jay
lay
lei
ley
may
nay
nee
neigh
pay
play
pray
ray
re
say
shay
slay

sleigh
spay
splay
spray
stay
stray
sway
they
tray
trey
way
weigh
whey
yea

(2)
affray
allay
array
assay
astray
away
aweigh
ballet
belay
beret
betray
bidet
blasé
bluejay
bouquet
buffet
cachet
café
chalet
chassé
cliché
convey
coupé

crochet
croquet
decay
defray
delay
dismay
display
doorway
entrée
épée
essay
estray
exray
filet
foray
forestay
frappé
frisé
gainsay
gourmet
inlay
inveigh
Kibei
lamé
leeway
maguey
mainstay
margay
massé
metier
midday
midway
misplay
moiré
moray
névé
Nisei
obey
outlay

outstay
outweigh
parfait
parlay
parquet
passé
piqué
portray
prepay
purvey
relay
repay
replay
risqué
roquet
roué
sachet
sashay
sauté
survey
touché
toupee
unlay
unsay
valet
waylay

(3)
anyway
applique
attaché
cabaret
caraway
castaway
consommé
cutaway
disobey
dossier
dubonnet

emigré
exposé
fiancé
fiancée
getaway
interplay
matinee
naiveté
negligee
overlay
overplay
passageway
photoplay
reconvey
resumé
ricochet
roundelay
sobriquet
underlay
underplay
virelay
waterway
yesterday

AB

blab
cab
crab
dab
drab
gab
grab
jab
lab
nab
scab
slab
stab

tab

(3)
baobab
taxicab

ACE

ace
base
brace
case
chase
dace
dais
face
grace
lace
mace
pace
place
race
space
trace
vase

(2)
abase
apace
debase
deface
disgrace
displace
efface
embrace
encase
enchase
enlace
erase

4

grimace
lipase
millrace
misplace
reface
replace
retrace
unbrace
unlace

(3)
contrabass
interface

ACK
back
black
brach
clack
claque
crack
flak
hack
jack
knack
lac
lack
pack
plaque
quack
rack
sac
sack
sacque
shack
slack
smack
snack

stack
tack
thwack
track
wack
wrack
yak

(2)
aback
attack
knapsack
knicknack
repack
retrack
unpack

(3)
almanac
amphibrach
bivouac
crackerjack
huckaback
iliac
leatherback
lumberjack
maniac
minitrack
oomiac
paddywhack
paperback
pickaback
piggyback
razorback
sandarac
tamarack
turtleback
zodiac

ACT
act
bract
fact
pact
tact
tract

(2)
abstract
attract
compact
contact
contract
detract
diffract
distract
enact
exact
extract
impact
infract
intact
protract
react
redact
refract
retract
transact

(3)
artifact
cataract
counteract
inexact
interact
underact

bad
bade
brad
cad
clad
dad
fad
gad
glad
grad
had
lad
mad
pad
plaid
sad
shad
tad

(2)
egad
forbade
gonad
monad
naiad
nomad
octad
unclad

(3)
aoudad
chiliad
hebdomad
ogdoad
oread

ade
aid
aide
bayed
blade
brade
braid
brayed
cade
fade
flayed
frayed
glade
hade
jade
lade
laid
made
maid
neighed
paid
played
prayed
preyed
raid
shade
spade
spayed
splayed
sprayed
staid
stayed
strayed
trade
wade
weighed

afraid
arcade
arrayed
assayed
betrayed
brocade
cascade
charade
conveyed
crusade
decayed
defrayed
degrade
dismayed
displayed
dissuade
downgrade
evade
inlaid
invade
inveighed
mermaid
obeyed
parade
parlayed
passade
persuade
pervade
pomade
portrayed
prepaid
relayed
repaid
torsade
unbraid
unlaid
unpaid

upbraid
upgrade
waylaid

(3)
accolade
aquacade
balustrade
barricade
bastinade
cannonade
cavalcade
centigrade
colonnade
defilade
dragonnade
enfilade
escalade
escapade
fusillade
gasconade
lemonade
marinade
marmalade
masquerade
palisade
parlormaid
pasquinade
prominade
readymade
renegade
retrograde
serenade
underlaid

AFE

chafe
safe

strafe
waif

(2)
unsafe
vouchsafe

AFF

baff
calf
chaff
daff
gaff
graph
half
laugh
quaff
sclaff
staff
waff

(2)
agraffe
behalf
carafe
digraph
distaff
mooncalf
paraph
restaff

(3)
allograph
altigraph
autograph
centotaph
dictograph
micrograph
monograph

odograph
shandygaff

AFT

aft
craft
daft
draft
draught
gaffed
graft
haft
kraft
raft
shaft
staffed
waft

(2)
abaft
aircraft
engraft
indraft
redraft
restaffed

(3)
autographed
countershaft
handicraft
overdraft
watercraft

AG

bag
brag
crag

drag
fag
flag
gag
hag
jag
lag
nag
quag
rag
sag
scrag
shag
slag
snag
sprag
stag
swag
tag
wag

(2)
mailbag
zigzag

(3)
bullyrag
carpetbag
scallawag

AGE

age
cage
gage
gauge
page
rage
sage
stage

swage
wage

(2)
assuage
downstage
encage
enrage
offstage
outrage
restage
upstage

(3)
archimage
disengage
underage

AINT

faint
feint
paint
plaint
quaint
saint
taint

(2)
acquaint
attaint
complaint
constraint
distraint
repaint
restraint

AIR

air
bare

bear
blare
care
chair
dare
ere
fare
flair
flare
glair
glare
hair
hare
heir
lair
mare
pair
pare
pear
prayer
rare
scare
share
snare
spare
square
stair
stare
swear
tare
tear
their
there
vair
ware
where

(2)
affair

aware
beware
compare
declare
despair
éclair
ensnare
forbear
forswear
foursquare
impair
nightmare
outstare
outwear
prepare
repair
unbear

(3)
agateware
anywhere
billionaire
debonaire
disrepair
doctrinaire
earthenware
legionnaire
lusterware
maidenhair
millionaire
overbear
questionnaire
silverware
thoroughfare
unaware
willowware

AKE

ache

bake
brake
break
cake
crake
drake
fake
flake
jake
lake
make
quake
rake
sake
shake
slake
snake
stake
steak
strake
take
wake

(2)
awake
betake
forsake
intake
lapstrake
mandrake
mistake
muckrake
namesake
opaque
partake
remake
retake
unmake

(3)
griddlecake
johnnycake
kittiwake
overtake
rattlesnake
undertake

AL

gal
pal
sal
shall

(2)
banal
canal
corral
decal
locale
morale
percale

(3)
musicale
rationale

ALE

ail
ale
bail
bale
brail
braille
dale
fail
flail
frail

gale
grail
hail
hale
jail
kale
mail
male
nail
pail
pale
quail
rail
sail
sale
scale
shale
snail
stale
swale
tail
tale
trail
vail
vale
veil
wail
wale
whale

(2)
assail
avail
bewail
blackmail
derail
detail
engrail
entail

exhale
impale
inhale
prevail
regale
retail
tenaille
unveil

(3)
bristletail
countervail
farthingale
intervale
martingale
monorail
nightingale
ponytail
swallowtail
tattletale

ALL

all
awl
ball
bawl
brawl
call
caul
crawl
drawl
fall
gall
hall
haul
mall
maul
pall
pawl

rall
scrawl
shawl
small
spall
sprawl
squall
stall
tall
thrall
trawl
wall
waul
yawl

(2)
appall
befall
catfall
deadfall
downfall
enthrall
forestall
install
landfall
nutgall
outfall
recall
withall

(3)
caterwaul
disenthrall
overhaul
thundersquall
waterfall

ALM

balm

calm
malm
palm
psalm
qualm

(2)
becalm
embalm
napalm

ALT

fault
halt
malt
salt
smalt
vault

(2)
asphalt
assault
basalt
default
exalt

(3)
somersault

AM

am
cam
clam
cram
dam
damn
dram
flam
gam

gram
ham
jam
jamb
lam
lamb
pam
pram
ram
scram
sham
slam
swam
tam
tram

(3)
aerogram
anagram
cablegram
cartogram
centigram
choriamb
chronogram
cofferdam
cryptogram
decagram
dithyramb
epigram
hexigram
kologram
logogram
microgram
monogram
pentagram
phonogram
seismogram
telegram
tetragram

AME

aim
blame
came
claim
dame
fame
flame
frame
game
hame
lame
maim
name
same
shame
tame

(2)
acclaim
aflame
became
bename
declaim
defame
disclaim
exclaim
inflame
misname
reclaim
rename

AMP

amp
camp
champ
clamp
cramp

damp
lamp
ramp
scamp
stamp
tamp
tramp
vamp

(2)
decamp
encamp
revamp

(3)
afterdamp
aide-de-camp

AN

an
ban
bran
can
clan
fan
gan
man
pan
panne
plan
ran
scan
span
tan
than
van

(2)
began
cancan

divan
japan
moulin
rattan
reman
saran
tisane
trepan
unman

(3)
caravan

ANCE

chance
dance
glance
grants
lance
manse
pants
plants
prance
rance
rants
slants
stance
trance

(2)
advance
askance
bechance
enhance
entrance
expanse
mischance
ordnance
perchance

romance

(3)
abeyance
acceptance
accordance
acquaintance
admittance
affiance
alliance
assonance
assurance
attendance
circumstance
cognizance
compliance
concordance
consonance
dalliance
defiance
dissonance
disturbance
elegance
encumbrance
endurance
expectance
flamboyance
furtherance
happenstance
hesitance
ignorance
importance
jubilance
miscreance
obeisance
observance
ordinance
petulance
pursuance

purtenance
purveyance
radiance
redundance
relevance
reliance
reluctance
remembrance
remittance
remonstrance
renaissance
repentance
repugnance
resemblance
resistance
resonance
severance
sibilance
sufferance
suppliance
surveilance
sustenance
temperance
tolerance
unbalance
utterance
variance
vigilance

ANCH

blanch
branch
ranch
stanch

(3)
anabranch
avalanche

AND

and
band
banned
bland
brand
canned
fanned
gland
grand
hand
land
manned
panned
planned
rand
sand
scanned
spanned
stand
strand
tanned

(2)
command
demand
disband
expand
gourmand
lowland
remand
withstand

(3)
allemande
ampersand
borderland
confirmand
contraband

countermand
deodand
fatherland
hinterland
overhand
overland
reprimand
tableland
underhand
understand
wonderland

ANE

bane
blain
brain
cane
chain
crane
deign
drain
fain
fane
feign
gain
grain
lain
lane
main
mane
pain
pane
plain
plane
rain
reign
rein
sain

sane
seine
skein
slain
sprain
stain
strain
swain
tain
thane
train
twain
vain
wane

(2)
abstain
arcane
arraign
attain
campaign
champagne
champaign
chicane
cocaine
complain
contain
delaine
demesne
deraign
detain
disdain
distrain
domain
enchain
engrain
enplane
entrain
explain

fusain
inane
ingrain
insane
maintain
membrane
methane
moraine
mortmain
mundane
murrain
obtain
ordain
pertain
profane
ptomaine
refrain
regain
remain
restrain
retain
sustain
terrain
terrane
urbane

(3)
aeroplane
afterpain
allophane
appertain
aquaplane
ascertain
cellophane
chatelaine
counterpane
entertain
featherbrain
foreordain

gyroplane
hurricane
hydroplane
inhumane
monoplane
preordain
rattlebrain
scatterbrain
suzerain
windowpane

(4)
legerdemain

ANG

bang
clang
fang
gang
hang
pang
rang
sang
slang
sprang
twang
whang

(2)
defang
harangue
linsang
mustang
rehang
shebang
trepang

(3)
boomerang
overhang

ANGE

change
grange
mange
range
strange

(2)
arrange
derange
estrange
exchange
outrange

(3)
disarrange
interchange
misarrange
prearrange

ANK

bank
blank
clank
crank
dank
drank
flank
franc
frank
hank
lank
plank
prank
rank
sank
shank
shrank
slank
spank
stank
swank
thank
yank

ANT

ant
aunt
brant
cant
chant
grant
pant
plant
rant
scant
slant

(2)
arrant
askant
aslant
decant
descant
displant
enchant
extant
gallant
implant
mutant
octant
regrant
replant
supplant
transplant

AP

cap
chap
clap
crap
dap
flap
frap
gap
hap
knap
lap
map
nap
pap
rap
sap
scrap
slap
snap
strap
tap
trap
wrap
yap

(2)
blackcap
claptrap
dewlap
entrap
lagniappe
kidnap
madcap
mishap
nightcap
recap
remap
uncap

unsnap
unstrap
unwrap

(3)
gingersnap
handicap
overlap
photomap
rattletrap
thunderclap

APE

ape
cape
chape
crape
crepe
drape
gape
grape
jape
nape
rape
scape
scrape
shape
tape

(2)
agape
escape
landscape

APSE

lapse

(2)
adapts

elapse
collapse
perhaps
prolapse
relapse
synapse

APT

apt
rapt
wrapt

(2)
adapt
enrapt.
inapt

AR

are
bar
car
char
czar
far
gar
jar
mar
par
scar
spar
star
tar
tsar

(2)
afar
bazaar
bizarre

boudoir
cigar
crossbar
daystar
debar
dinar
disbar
guitar
instar
jacktar
jaguar
lodestar
memoir

(3)
abattoir
avatar
caviar
commissar
escritoire
insofar
registrar
repertoire
seminar

ARCH

arch
larch
march
parch
starch

ARD

bard
barred
card
chard
charred

guard
hard
lard
marred
nard
sard
shard
starred
tarred
yard

(2)
canard
discard
dooryard
mansard
petard
regard
retard

(3)
boulevard
disregard
interlard
leotard
lumberyard

ARE/EAR
as in
bare/bear
(see AIR)

ARGE
barge
charge
large
sarge
targe

(2)
discharge
enlarge
recharge
surcharge

ARK
arc
ark
bark
barque
dark
hark
lark
marc
mark
marque
nark
park
shark
snark
spark
stark

(2)
debark
embark
impark
remark
remarque

(3)
disembark
matriarch
oligarch
patriarch

ARM
arm

barm
charm
farm
harm

(2)
alarm
disarm

ARP
carp
harp
scarp
sharp

ART
art
cart
carte
chart
dart
hart
heart
mart
part
quarte
smart
start
tart

(2)
apart
athwart
compart
depart
dispart
impart
outsmart
oxheart

upstart

(3)
a la carte
counterpart

ASH

ash
bash
brash
cache
cash
clash
crash
dash
flash
gash
gnash
hash
lash
mash
rash
sash
slash
smash
stash
thrash
trash

(2)
abash
backlash
calash
eyelash
mustache
panache
rehash

(3)
balderdash

calabash
succotash

ASK

ask
bask
basque
cask
casque
flask
mask
masque
task

ASP

asp
clasp
gasp
grasp
hasp
rasp

(2)
unclasp

ASS

ass
bass
brass
class
crass
gas
glass
grass
lass
mass
pass

sass

(2)
alas
amass
crevasse
jackass
morass
outclass
repass
surpass

(3)
fiberglass
interclass
isinglass
overpass
peppergrass
plexiglass
sassafras
underpass

AST

bast
blast
cast
caste
fast
hast
last
mast
past
vast

(2)
aghast
amassed
avast
contrast
dismast

downcast
mainmast
miscast
outcast
recast
repast
surpassed

(3)
archiblast
counterblast
flabbergast
metaphrast
mizzenmast
overcast
telecast

ASTE

baste
braced
cased
chased
chaste
graced
haste
laced
maced
paced
paste
placed
raced
spaced
taste
traced
waist
waste

(2)
abased

defaced
disgraced
distaste
effaced
embraced
encased
impaste
lambaste
posthaste
retraced
unchaste

AT

at
bat
batt
blat
brat
cat
chat
drat
fat
flat
frat
gat
gnat
hat
mat
matte
pat
plait
plat
prat
rat
sat
scat
slat
spat

splat
sprat
tat
that
vat

(2)
begat
chitchat
cravat
muskrat
therat

(3)
acrobat
autocrat
automat
bureaucrat
butterfat
caveat
democrat
diplomat
habitat
hydrostat
marrowfat
monocrat
photostat
rheostat
thermostat

ATCH

batch
catch
cratch
hatch
latch
match
patch
scratch

snatch
thatch

(2)
attach
crosshatch
detach
dispatch
mismatch
nuthatch
outmatch
rematch
unlatch

ATE
ate
bait
bate
crate
date
eight
fate
fete
freight
gait
gate
grate
great
hate
late
mate
pate
plate
prate
rate
sate
skate
slate

spate
state
straight
strait
trait
wait
weight

(2)
abate
await
berate
create
debate
deflate
delate
dilate
distrait
elate
equate
estate
inflate
innate
instate
irate
locate
mismate
narrate
oblate
orate
ornate
postdate
predate
relate
restate
rotate
sedate
translate
update

(3)
abdicate
abrogate
activate
aggravate
agitate
alienate
allocate
animate
antedate
arbitrate
aspirate
automate
calculate
calibrate
candidate
captivate
castigate
celebrate
celibate
circulate
compensate
complicate
concentrate
confiscate
congregate
consecrate
culminate
cultivate
decimate
decorate
dedicate
delegate
desolate
detonate
devastate
dislocate
dominate
educate

elevate	mediate	vegetate
emulate	medicate	venerate
enervate	meditate	ventilate
estimate	mitigate	vindicate
excavate	motivate	violate
expiate	mutilate	vitiate
expurgate	nominate	
fabricate	obfuscate	ATH
fascinate	obligate	bath
flagellate	ordinate	hath
fumigate	oscillate	lath
generate	penetrate	math
germinate	percolate	snath
hesitate	permeate	wrath
hibernate	perpetrate	strath
hyphenate	postulate	
illustrate	potentate	(2)
imitate	predicate	bypath
immigrate	profligate	
implicate	propagate	(3)
indicate	punctuate	aftermath
insolate	radiate	allopath
instigate	relegate	bridlepath
insulate	renovate	
integrate	reprobate	AUD
intonate	roseate	bawd
invocate	simulate	broad
irrigate	speculate	fraud
irritate	stimulate	gaud
isolate	stipulate	laud
jubilate	strangulate	maud
lacerate	suffocate	
legislate	surrogate	(2)
levitate	syncopate	applaud
liberate	terminate	defraud
lineate	tolerate	maraud
litigate	vaccinate	
lubricate	vacillate	AUGHT
magistrate	validate	(see OUGHT)

AUNCH

haunch
launch
paunch
staunch

AUNT

chaunt
daunt
flaunt
gaunt
haunt
jaunt
taunt
vaunt

AUSE

cause
caws
clause
gauze
hawse
pause

(2)
applause
because
inlaws
jackdaws
jackstraws

AVE

brave
cave
crave
gave

grave
knave
lave
nave
pave
save
shave
slave
stave
trave
waive
wave

(2)
behave
concave
conclave
deprave
enclave
enslave
forgave
margrave
octave
repave

(3)
architrave
autoclave
microwave
misbehave

AWE

awe
caw
chaw
claw
draw
flaw
gnaw

haw
jaw
law
maw
paw
raw
saw
shaw
slaw
squaw
straw
tau
taw
thaw

(2)
coleslaw
cushaw
dewclaw
gewgaw
inlaw
jackstraw
jigsaw
lockjaw
macaw
outlaw
papaw
pilaw
withdraw

AWK

auk
balk
calk
chalk
gawk
hawk
squawk

22

stalk
talk
walk

(2)
crosswalk
jaywalk

AWN

awn
brawn
dawn
drawn
faun
fawn
gone
lawn
on
pawn
prawn
spawn
yawn

(2)
begone
foregone
upon
withdrawn

(3)
leprechaun

AZE

baise
bays
blaze
braise
brays

braze
chaise
clays
craze
days
daze
drays
faze
flays
frays
gaze
grays
graze
haze
lays
laze
leis
maize
maze
phase
phrase
praise
prase
prays
raise
raze

(3)
anaphase
metaphase
metaphrase
overglaze
overlays
paraphrase

AZH

(2)
barrage

collage
corsage
garage
massage
menage
mirage
moulage

(3)
bon voyage
comouflage
curettage
entourage
espionage
fusilage
persiflage

AFTER SLEEPING . . .

That afternoon,
near a small pond,
I saw it sleeping
in seedpods.

Taking one of them
in my hand,
the loss of a loved
one was explained.

After a season
of sleeping,
seeds burst their
encasement, giving
forth new life.

—nm

23

ABBER

(2)
blabber
clabber
crabber
dabber
gabber
jabber
stabber
yabber

ABBLE

(2)
babble
brabble
dabble
drabble
gabble
grabble
rabble
scrabble

ABBY

(2)
cabby
flabby
gabby
scabby
shabby
tabby

ABLE

(2)
able
cable
fable
gable
label
labile
sable
table

ABOR

(2)
labor
neighbor
saber
tabor

(3)
belabor

ACEOUS

(2)
gracious
spacious

(3)
fallacious
loquacious
mendacious
rapacious
sagacious
salacious
tenacious
veracious
vivacious
voracious

ACITY

(4)
audacity
capacity
feracity
fugacity
mendacity
mordacity
opacity
predacity
pugnacity
rapacity
sagacity
salacity
tenacity
veracity
voracity

(5)
perspicacity
pertinacity

ACKER

(3)
backer
blacker
cracker
knacker
lacquer
packer
sacker
slacker
smacker
stacker
tacker
tracker

(3)
bushwhacker
firecracker
hijacker
linebacker

ACKLE

(2)
cackle

24

crackle
grackle
hackle
jackal
mackle
macle
shackle
tackle

(3)
debacle
ramshackle
unshackle

(4)
tabernacle

ACTION

(2)
action
faction
fraction
taction
traction

(3)
abstraction
attraction
compaction
contraction
detraction
distraction
enaction
extraction
impaction
olfaction
protraction
reaction
redaction
refraction

retraction
transaction

ACTOR

(2)
actor
factor
tractor

(3)
protractor
reactor
redactor
transaction

(4)
malefactor

ADDER

(2)
adder
bladder
gadder
ladder
madder
sadder

ADDLE

(2)
addle
paddle
raddle
saddle
staddle
straddle

(3)
astraddle
bestraddle

packsaddle
sidesaddle
skedaddle

AGGLE

(2)
draggle
haggle
straggle
waggle

(3)
bedraggle

AGGY

(2)
baggy
craggy
shaggy
snaggy

AILER

(2)
jailer
mailer
paler
sailor
tailor
trailer
whaler

AINER

(2)
gainer
plainer
planer
saner

seiner
strainer
vainer

(3)
abstainer
campaigner
complainer
container
detainer
distrainor
half gainer
restrainer
retainer

AKER

(2)
acre
baker
breaker
faker
fakir
maker
nacre
quaker
shaker
slaker
snaker
taker

(3)
bookmaker
glassmaker
heartbreaker
icebreaker
matchmaker
pacemaker
partaker

peacemaker
safebreaker
speechmaker
strikebreaker
toolmaker
windbreaker
wiseacre

ALITY

(4)
banality
brutality
finality
formality
frugality
locality
mentality
normality
rascality
regality
sodality
spectrality
tonality
venality
vitality
vocality

ALLIC

(2)
phallic
thallic

(3)
medallic
metallic
oxallic

ALLION

(2)
scallion
stallion

(3)
medallion
rapscallion

ALLOW

(2)
fallow
hallow
mallow
sallow
shallow
tallow

(3)
marshmallow

AMBLE

(2)
amble
bramble
gamble
ramble
scramble
shamble

(3)
preamble
unscramble

AMMER

(2)
clamor
grammar

hammer
rammer
shammer
slammer
stammer
yammer

(3)
triphammer
windjammer

AMPER

(2)
camper
clamper
damper
hamper
pamper
scamper
tamper

AMPLE
(2)
ample
sample
trample

(3)
example

ANCER

(2)
cancer
dancer
lancer
prancer

(3)
enhancer

freelancer
romancer
ropedancer

ANDER

(2)
candor
gander
pander
sander
slander

(3)
germander
goosander
meander
philander
pomander
woodlander

(4)
calamander
gerrymander
oleander
salamander

ANDLE

(2)
candle
dandle
handle
sandal
vandal

(3)
manhandle
mishandle
panhandle

ANDY

(2)
bandy
brandy
candy
dandy
handy
sandy

ANGER

(2)
anger
clangor
ganger
hanger
languor

(3)
straphanger

ANGLE

(2)
angle
bangle
dangle
jangle
mangle
strangle
tangle
wangle
wrangle

(3)
embrangle
entangle
octangle
quadrangle
rectangle

triangle
untangle

ANGLER

(2)
angler
dangler
jangler
mangler
tangler
wangler
wrangler

ANIC

(2)
manic
panic
stannic
tannic

(3)
galvanic
melanic
morganic
organic
satanic
shamanic
tetanic
tympanic
tyrannic
uranic
volcanic

(4)
puritanic

ANISH

(2)
banish
clannish
mannish
vanish

ANJER

(2)
danger
granger
manger
ranger
stranger

ANKER

(2)
anchor
banker
chancre
cranker
flanker
hanker
rancor
ranker
spanker

ANNER

(2)
banner
canner
fanner
manner
planner
scanner
spanner
tanner

ANTER

(2)
banter
canter
cantor
chanter
grantor
planter

(3)
decanter
trochanter

(4)
covenanter
gallivanter

ANTIC

(2)
antic
frantic
mantic

(3)
gigantic
pedantic
romantic
semantic

APER

(2)
caper
draper
paper
raper
scraper
shaper

taper
tapir
vapor

(3)
flypaper
newspaper
oilpaper
sandpaper
skyscraper
wallpaper
wastepaper

APPER

(2)
capper
clapper
dapper
flapper
lapper
napper
rapper
scrapper
slapper
snapper
strapper
tapper
trapper
wrapper

(3)
backslapper
kidnapper

(4)
handicapper
whippersnapper

APPY

(2)
crappie
happy
nappy
pappy
sappy
scrappy
snappy

ARITY

(3)
charity
clarity
parity
rarity

(4)
barbarity
disparity
hilarity
imparity
polarity

ARKER

(2)
barker
darker
marker
parker
starker

ARMER

(2)
armor
charmer
farmer

ARROW

(2)
arrow
barrow
farrow
harrow
narrow
sparrow
yarrow

ARRY

(2)
aerie
airy
carry
chary
clary
fairy
hairy
harry
marry

ARTER

(2)
barter
carter
charter
darter
garter
martyr
smarter
starter
tarter

ARY

(3)
contrary

library
primary
rosemary

(4)
apiary
arbitrary
budgetary
capillary
cinerary
commissary
coronary
culinary
customary
dictionary
dietary
emissary
estuary
formicary
fragmentary
functionary
funerary
honorary
lapidary
literary
luminary
mercenary
military
millenary
missionary
monetary
necessary
numerary
ordinary
ovulary
papillary
pigmentary
planetary
pulmonary

quaternary
reliquary
salivary
salutary
sanctuary
sanguinary
sanitary
secretary
sedentary
segmentary
seminary
solitary
statuary
sumptuary
syllabary
temporary
tertiary
titulary
topiary
tributary
tutelary
unitary
vespiary
visionary
voluntary

(5)
contemporary
conversionary
deflationary
extemporary
hereditary
imaginary
itinerary
judiciary
obituary
pecuniary
precautionary
preliminary

proprietary
provisionary
reactionary
tercentenary
veterinary
vocabulary

ASHER

(2)
dasher
flasher
masher
rasher
splasher
thrasher

(4)
haberdasher

ASION

(2)
nasion
suasion

(3)
corrasion
dissuasion
invasion
occasion
persuasion
pervasion

ASSION

(2)
fashion
passion
ration

(3)
dispassion

ASTER

(2)
aster
caster
faster
master
pastor
plaster
raster
vaster

(3)
diaster
disaster
forecaster
headmaster
paymaster
piaster
ringmaster
schoolmaster
scoutmaster
shinplaster
shipmaster
taskmaster
trainmaster
yardmaster

ATHER

(2)
blather
gather
lather
rather
slather

ATIC

(2)
static

(3)
asmatic
climatic
dogmatic
dramatic
emphatic
erratic
fanatic
hepatic
magmatic
phlegmatic
pneumatic
pragmatic
prismatic
schematic
schismatic
somatic
stigmatic
stomatic
thematic
traumatic

(4)
acrobatic
automatic
enigmatic
mathematic
morganatic
numismatic
operatic
photostatic
problematic
symptomatic
systematic
technocratic
theocratic

ATION

(2)
nation
ration
station

(3)
creation
deflation
dilation
inflation
lavation
legation
libation
ligation
location
migration
mutation
narration
negation
notation
oblation
oration
ovation
privation
prostration
quotation
relation
rotation
salvation
sensation
stagnation
starvation
summation
taxation
temptation
translation
vacation
vibration

vocation

ATOR

(2)
baiter
cater
dater
gaiter
hater
later
mater
pater
satyr
slater
traitor
waiter

(3)
abater
delator
dictator
dilator
headwaiter
levator
migrator
pulsator
relator
rotator
spectator
testator
tidewaiter
translator
vibrator

(4)
elevator
indicator
innovator
legislator

liberator
lubricator
meditator
navigator
numerator
operator
oscillator
perpetrator
postulator
propagator
radiator
regulator
renovator
respirator
revelator
ruminator
simulator
speculator
stimulator
subjagator
syncopator
tabulator
terminator
ventilator
vindicator
violater
vitiator

ATTER

(2)
attar
batter
chatter
clatter
fatter
flatter
hatter
latter

matter
patter
platter
ratter
scatter
shatter
smatter
spatter
splatter
tatter

(3)
bespatter
standpatter
wildcatter

ATTLE

(2)
battle
cattle
chattel
prattle
rattle
tattle

AVEL

(2)
cavil
gavel
gravel
ravel
travel

AVER

(2)
favor
flavor
laver

32

paver
quaver
raver
saver
savor
shaver
slaver
waiver
waver

AVITY

(3)
cavity
gravity

(4)
concavity
depravity

AZER

(2)
blazer
hazer
laser
maser
razor

(3)
stargazer

AZY

(2)
crazy
daisy
hazy
lazy
mazy

E

be
bee
bree
cay
cee
dee
di
fee
fi
flea
flee
free
gee
ghee
glee
gree
he
key
knee
lea
lee
li
me
mi
pea
plea
quay
re
scree
sea
see
she
si
ski
spree
tea
tee
thee
three
ti
tree
vee
we
wee
whee
ye
zee

(2)
agree
alea
banshee
debris
decree
degree
esprit
foresee
grandee
killdee
lessee
levee
machree
marquee
mustee

One's writing is good only where the intelligence and the imagination are in equilibrium. As soon as one of them over-balances the other, it is all up.
—Tolstoy

ogee
payee
pollee
pongee
postfree
précis
settee
spondee
standee
vendee
whangee

(3)
absentee
addressee
alienee
amputee
apogee
appellee
axletree
bumblebee
calipee
chimpanzee
conferee
coterie
deportee
designee
devotee
disagree
doubletree
dungaree
epopee
filigree
fricassee
garnishee
gaucherie
guarantee
inductee
jamboree

jubilee
legatee
manatee
manteltree
metope
mortgagee
nominee
obligee
oversee
patentee
pedigree
referee
refugee
separtee
sangaree
simile
stingaree
syncope
systole
trestletree
undersea
warantee

EACH

beach
beech
bleach
breech
each
leach
leech
peach
pleach
preach
reach
screech
speech
teach

(2)
beseech
impeach
outreach

EAD (see EED)
EAK (see EEK)
EAL (see EEL)
EAM (see EEM)
EAN (see EEN)
EAP (see EEP)
EAR (see EER)
EASE (see EZ)

EAST

beast
east
feast
least
priest
yeast

(2)
artiste
batiste
modiste

EAT (see EET)

EATH

heath
sheath
teeth
wreath

(2)
beneath
bequeath

EATHE

breathe
seethe
sheathe
teethe
wreathe

ECE

cease
crease
fleece
geese
grease
lease
niece
peace
piece

(2)
apiece
caprice
cerise
decease
decrease
increase
obese
police
release
sublease
valise

(3)
afterpiece
altarpiece
ambergris
centerpiece
diocese
frontispiece
mantelpiece

masterpiece

ECK

check
deck
fleck
neck
peck
speck
wreck

(2)
bedeck
poopdeck

(3)
afterdeck
bottleneck
countercheck
discotheque
overcheck
rubberneck
turtleneck

ECT

sect

(2)
abject
affect
bisect
collect
connect
correct
defect
deflect
deject
detect
direct

dissect
effect
eject
elect
erect
expect
exsect
infect
insect
inspect
neglect
object
perfect
prefect
prelect
project
protect
refect
reflect
reject
resect
select
subject
transect

(3)
architect
circumspect
dialect
disconnect
disrespect
genuflect
incorrect
indirect
intellect
interject
intersect
introspect
quadrisect

recollect
retrospect
vivisect

ED

bed
bled
bread
bred
dead
dread
fed
fled
head
lead
led
pled
read
red
said
shed
shred
sled
sped
spread
stead
ted
thread
tread
wed
zed

(2)
abed
ahead
behead
bobsled
embed
inbred

instead
masthead
outspread
retread

(3)
aliped
arrowhead
copperhead
dragonhead
featherbed
fiddlehead
fountainhead
gingerbread
hammerhead
infrared
loggerhead
milliped
multiped

EDGE

dredge
edge
fledge
hedge
kedge
ledge
pledge
sedge
sledge
wedge

EED

bead
bleed
brede
breed
cede

creed
deed
feed
freed
greed
heed
keyed
knead
lead
lied
mead
meed
need
plead
read
rede
reed
seed
screed
speed
steed
treed
tweed
weed

(2)
accede
agreed
concede
crossbreed
decreed
exceed
impede
inbreed
indeed
misdeed
mislead
moonseed
outbreed

precede
proceed
recede
secede
succeed
stampede

(3)
aniseed
antecede
beggarweed
bitterweed
bugleweed
centipede
colicweed
intercede
locoweed
millipede
multipede
pedigreed
retrocede
supersede
tumbleweed

EEF

beef
brief
chief
fief
grief
leaf
lief
reef
sheaf
thief

(2)
belief
debrief

metif
motif
naif
relief
sherif

(3)
cloverleaf
disbelief
interleaf
leitmotif
unbelief

EEK

beak
bleak
cheek
chic
cleek
clique
creak
creek
eke
freak
leak
leek
meek
peak
peek
pique
reek
screak
seek
shriek
sleek
sneak
squeak
streak
teak

weak
week
wreak

(2)
antique
batik
bespeak
critique
midweek
mistique
oblique

EEL

ceil
creel
deal
eel
feel
heal
heel
kneel
meal
peal
peel
real
reel
seal
spiel
squeal
steal
steel
teal
tuille
veal
weal
wheel
zeal

(2)
abele
anele
anneal
appeal
chenille
conceal
congeal
freewheel
ideal
misdeal
newsreel
oatmeal
ordeal
repeal
reveal

(3)
cockateel
commonweal
dishabille
goldenseal

EEM

beam
bream
cream
deem
dream
gleam
ream
scheme
scream
seam
seem
steam
stream
team

teem
theme

(2)
abeam
agleam
beseem
blaspheme
daydream
esteem
extreme
millstream
morpheme
redeem
supreme
upstream

EEN

bean
clean
dean
gene
glean
green
jean
keen
lean
lien
mean
mesne
mien
peen
preen
queen
seen
scene
screen
sheen
spleen

teen
ween

(2)
bemean
between
canteen
careen
convene
cuisine
demean
demesne
gangrene
lateen
machine
marine
obscene
ravine
routine
sardine
sateen
scalene
serene
terrene
tureen
unclean

(3)
evergreen
figurine
gabardine
gasoline
guillotine
intervene
kerosene
libertine
magazine
mezzanine
nectarine
nicotine

quarantine
serpentine
submarine
supervene
tambourine
wintergreen
wolverine

EEP

cheap
cheep
creep
deep
heap
jeep
keep
leap
neap
neep
peep
reap
seep
sheep
sleep
steep
sweep
weep

EER

beer
bier
blear
cere
cheer
clear
dear
drear
ear

fear
gear
hear
here
jeer
leer
mere
near
peer
pier
queer
rear
sear
seer
sere
shear
sheer
smear
sneer
spear
sphere
steer
stere
tear
tier
veer
weir
year

(2)

adhere
appear
austere
besmear
career
cashier
cashmere
cohere
compeer

endear
ensphere
inhere
revere
severe
sincere
unclear
veneer

(3)

atmosphere
bandoleer
bathysphere
belevedere
bombardier
brigadier
buccaneer
cavalier
chandelier
chanticleer
chiffonier
commandeer
disappear
domineer
engineer
gazeteer
grenadier
hemisphere
interfere
jardiniere
lavaliere
musketeer
mutineer
overhear
persevere
pioneer
racketeer
sonneteer
volunteer

EET

beat
beet
bleat
cheat
cleat
eat
feat
feet
fleet
greet
heat
meat
meet
mete
neat
peat
pleat
seat
sheet
skeet
sleet
street
suite
sweet
teat
treat
tweet
wheat

(2)
accrete
compete
complete
conceit
defeat
delete
deplete
discreet

downbeat
effete
elite
entreat
esthete
excrete
maltreat
mesquite
mistreat
petite
receipt
repeat
replete
reseat
retreat
secrete
unseat

(3)
bittersweet
exegete
incomplete
indiscreet
marguerite
meadowsweet
obsolete
overeat
overheat
paraclete
parakeet

EETH (see EATH)

EFT

cleft
deft
eft
klepht
left

theft
weft

(2)
bereft

EIGHT (see ATE)

ELD

geld
held
meld
weld

(2)
beheld
upheld

ĒLD

field
weald
wield
yield

(2)
airfield
backfield
infield
outfield

ELL

bell
belle
cell
dell
dwell
ell
fell
hell

jell
knell
mel
quell
sell
shell
smell
snell
spell
swell
tell
well
yell

(2)
befell
cartel
chandelle
compel
cordelle
dispel
excel
expel
foretell
gazelle
impel
lapel
morel
motel
nutshell
outshell
pastel
propel
quenelle
rebel
repel
upswell

(3)
asphodel

bagatelle
caravelle
carrousel
citadel
clientele
cockleshell
jargonelle
mademoiselle
oenomel
oversell
parallel
pimpernel
undersell

ELT

belt
celt
dealt
dwelt
elt
felt
gelt
knelt
melt
pelt
smelt
svelte

ELVES

delves
elves
helves
shelves
twelves

(2)
ourselves

themselves
yourselves

EM

creme
em
gem
hem
mem
phlegm
stem
them

(2)
ahem
condemn

(3)
anadem
apothegm
diadem
meristem
periblem

EN

been
den
en
fen
glen
hen
ken
men
pen
ten
then
wen
when
wren

yen

(2)
again
amen
cayenne

ENCE

pence
sense
spence
tense
thence
whence

(2)
commence
condense
defense
dispense
expense
immense
incense
intense
nascence
nonsense
offence
prepense
pretense
suspence

(3)
decadence
deference
dependence
deterrence
difference
diffidence
diligence
dissidence

divergence
divulgence
effluence
effulgence
eloquence
eminence
evidence
excellence
excrescence
frankincense
fraudulence
imminence
impotence
indigence
indolence
insistence
insolence
liquescence
negligence
occurrence
opulence
pentitence
permanence
persistence
pertinence
pestilence
preference
prescience
prominence
providence
prurience
quintessence
recompence
recurrence
redolence
reference
refulgence
renascence
repellence

residence
respondence
resurgence
reverence
salience
sapience
somnolence
subsistence
succulence
transcendence
transference
transparence
truculence
turbulence
vehemence
violence
virulence
vitrescence

ENCH

bench
clench
drench
quench
stench
trench
wench
wrench

(2)
entrench
retrench

END

bend
blend
end
fend

friend
lend
mend
pend
rend
scend
send
spend
tend
trend
vend
wend

(2)
addend
amend
append
ascend
attend
befriend
commend
contend
defend
depend
descend
dispend
distend
emend
expend
extend
impend
intend
misspend
offend
portend
perpend
pretend
resend
suspend

transcend
unbend
upend

(3)
apprehend
coextend
comprehend
condescend
dividend
recommend

ENT

bent
cent
dent
gent
lent
meant
pent
rent
scent
sent
spent
tent
vent
went

(2)
absent
anent
ascent
assent
augment
cement
concent
consent
content
dement

descent
detent
dissent
extent
ferment
foment
indent
intent
invent
lament
percent
portent
present
prevent
relent
repent
resent
unsent
unspent

(3)
circumvent
consequent
discontent
document
malcontent
ornament
pediment
penitent
permanent
pestilent
represent
sacrament
underwent

EPT

crept
kept
leapt

43

pepped
slept
stepped
wept

(2)
adept
accept
concept
except
incept
inept
transept
unswept
unwept
y-clept

(3)
intercept
nympholept

ER (see UR)
ERD (see URD)
ERE (see EER)
ERGE (see URGE)
ERM (see URM)
ERN (see URN)
ERSE (see URSE)
ERST (see URST)
ERT (see URT)
ERTH (see URTH)
ERVE (see URVE)

ESH

creche
flesh
fresh
mesh
thresh

(2)
afresh
enmesh
refresh

ESS

bless
cess
chess
cress
dress
ess
guess
less
mess
press
stress
tress
yes

(2)
address
aggress
assesss
caress
compress
confess
depress
digress
distress
duress
empress
excess
express
finesse
impress
obsess
oppress
possess

profess
progress
recess
redress
regress
repress
success
suppress
transgress
unless

(3)
acquiesce
coalesce
convalesce
decompress
deliquesce
dispossess
effervesce
evanesce
incandesce
luminesce
opalesce
overdress
prepossess
repossess
retrogress
watercress

EST

best
blest
breast
chest
crest
gest
guest
jest
lest

44

nest
pest
quest
rest
test
vest
west
wrest
zest

(2)
abreast
arrest
attest
behest
bequest
congest
conquest
contest
detest
digest
divest
impressed
incest
infest
ingest
inquest
invest
molest
protest
request
revest
suggest
unrest

(3)
alkahest
anapest
manifest

ET
bet
blet
debt
fret
get
jet
let
met
net
pet
set
stet
sweat
threat
wet
whet
yet

(2)
abet
barrette
beget
beset
brunet
brunette
cadet
casette
coquette
dinette
forget
gazette
georgette
inlet
inset
layette
lorgnette
moonset
motet

musette
nailset
offset
paillette
regret
reset
revet
rosette
roulette
sublet
tercet
upset

(3)
alphabet
avocet
bassinet
bayonet
calumet
canzonet
cigarette
clarinet
coronet
epithet
marmoset
martinet
mignonette
minaret
minuet
silhouette
triolet
vinaigrette

ETCH
etch
fetch
fletch
ketch
retch

sketch
stretch
vetch
wretch

(2)
backstretch
outstretch

ETE (see EET)

EVE

breve
cleave
eave
eve
grieve
heave
leave
peeve
reave
reeve
sheave
sleeve
steeve
thieve
weave

(2)
achieve
aggrieve
believe
bereave
conceive
deceive
naive
perceive
receive
relieve
reprieve

retrieve
unreeve
upheave

(3)
apperceive
disbelieve
interleave
interweave
misbelieve
misconceive
preconceive
semibreve

EX

flex
hex
rex
sex
vex

(2)
annex
apex
codex
complex
convex
cortex
culex
index
murex
narthex
perplex
reflex

(3)
circumflex
interrex
multiplex
oversex

pontiflex
quadruplex
retroflex
unisex

EZ

breeze
cheese
ease
feaze
freeze
frieze
lees
mise
pease
please
seize
squeeze
tease
these
tweeze
wheeze

(2)
appease
chemise
deepfreeze
disease
displease
trapeze

(3)
antifreeze
apices
litotes
matrices

(4)
appendices
isosceles

AS IF TO REMIND ME*

Lilies
Bloom, flourish, close
In one day, reminding
Me not to fritter a moment
Of time.

EACHER

(2)
bleacher
creature
feature
teacher
preacher

EADER (see EEDER)

EAGLE

(2)
beagle
eagle
legal
regal

EAKER (see EEKER)
EALER (see EELER)
EAMER (see EEMER)
EANER (see EENER)
EAPER (see EEPER)
EATER (see EETER)

EATHER

(2)
feather
heather
leather
tether
weather
wether
whether

(3)
pinfeather
together
whitleather

EAVEN

(2)
heaven
leaven
seven

(3)
eleven

EAVER (see EEVER)

ECTION

(2)
lection
section
vection

(3)
affection
confection
connection
convection
correction
defection
dejection
detection
direction
dissection
election
erection
infection
inflection
injection
prefection
prelection
projection
protection
reflection
rejection
resection
selection
subjection
transection

(4)
genuflection
insurrection
interjection
introspection
predilection
recollection
retrospection

* Rules for the cinquain are on page 116.

ECTIVE

(3)
affective
collective
connective
corrective
detective
effective
elective
invective
objective
selective

EDDLE

(2)
medal
meddle
pedal
peddle

EEDER

(2)
beader
bleeder
breeder
feeder
leader
reader
seeder
speeder
weeder

EEKER

(2)
beaker
meeker
peeker
seeker
sleeker
sneaker
speaker
squeaker
weaker

EELER

(2)
dealer
feeler
healer
peeler
sealer
wheeler

EEMER

(2)
creamer
dreamer
reamer
screamer
steamer

EENER

(2)
cleaner
gleaner
greener
keener
leaner
meaner
screener
wiener

(3)
demeanor
serener

EEPER

(2)
creeper
deeper
keeper
leaper
peeper
reaper
sleeper
steeper
weeper

(3)
beekeeper
bookkeeper
housekeeper
shopkeeper
storekeeper
tollkeeper

EETER

(2)
beater
cheater
eater
greeter
heater
liter
meter
neater
pleater
sweeter
teeter
tweeter

(3)
repeater
saltpeter
toadeater

EEVER

(2)
beaver
cleaver
fever
heaver
lever
weaver
weever

(3)
achiever
believer
deceiver
perceiver
receiver
retriever

ELLER

(2)
cellar
dweller
feller
heller
seller
sheller
smeller
speller
stellar
teller

(3)
propeller
rathskeller
repeller
saltcellar

ELLOW

(2)
bellow
cello
fellow
mellow
yellow

(3)
yokefellow

ELTER

(2)
shelter
smelter
spelter
welter

(4)
helter-skelter

ENDER

(2)
bender
blender
ender
fender
gender
lender
mender
render
sender
slender
spender
splendor
tender
vendor

(3)
contender
defender
descender
hellbender
surrender

ENTAL

(2)
dental
gentle
lentil
mental
rental

(3)
parental
segmental

(4)
alimental
detrimental
documental
elemental
fundamental
governmental
implemental
instrumental
monumental
occidental
oriental
ornamental
pedimental
regimental
rudimental
sacramental
sedimental
sentimental
supplemental

ENTER

(2)
center
mentor
renter
tenter

(3)
assenter
dissenter
presenter
tormentor

(4)
circumventer
documenter
epicenter

ENTION

(2)
gentian
mention
pension
tension

(3)
abstention
ascension
contention
convention
declension
dimension
dissension
distension
extension
indention
intention
invention
pretension

prevention
recension
retention
suspension

(4)
apprehension
circumvention
comprehension
condescension

ENTURE

(2)
censure
denture
venture

(3)
adventure
debenture
indenture

EPTION

(3)
conception
deception
exception
inception
perception
reception

ERIC

(2)
cleric
ferric
steric

(3)
esoteric

exoteric
glyceric
mesmeric
turmeric
valeric

(4)
hemispheric
metameric
tautomeric

ERIOR

(4)
anterior
exterior
inferior
interior
posterior
superior
ulterior

ERITY

(3)
verity

(4)
prosperity
temerity
severity
sincerity

ERRY

(2)
berry
bury
cherry
derry
ferry

merry
very

(4)
lamasery
mesentery
monastery

ESSION

(2)
session

(3)
concession
confession
degression
depression
digression
discretion
egression
expression
obsession
oppression
possession
precession
procession
profession
progression
recession
regression
succession
suppression
transgression

ESSOR

(2)
dresser
lesser
pressor

(3)
assessor
compressor
confessor
oppressor
successor

ESTER

(3)
attester
digester
investor
molester
northwester
semester
sequester
southwester
trimester

ETIC

(3)
ascetic
heretic
hermetic
magnetic
mimetic
paretic
pathetic
phonetic
phrenetic
prophetic
splenetic
syncretic
synthetic
tonetic

(4)
apathetic
dietetic
energetic
epithetic
geodetic
kinesthetic
parenthetic
paresthetic
sympathetic
synergetic

ESTLE

(2)
nestle
pestle
trestle
vessel
wrestle

ETION

(3)
completion
deletion
depletion
excretion
impletion
incretion
repletion
secretion

ETTER

(2)
better
debtor
fetter
letter
setter

sweater
wetter
whetter

(3)
begetter
forgetter
go-getter
typesetter
unfetter
vignetter

ETTLE

(2)
fettle
kettle
metal
mettle
nettle
petal
settle

EVEL

(2)
bevel
devil
level
revel

(3)
bedevil
dishevel

EVER

(2)
clever
ever
lever

never
sever

LANTERNE SEQUENCE*

Bird
tracks on
wet sand: dance
steps for happy
child.
***
Fall's
first grand
marshal of
color marches
by.
***
Full
moons with
stars cannot
make the light of
day.

—nm

I
ai
aye
buy
by
bye
cry
die
dry
dye
eye
fie

fly
fry
guy
hie
high
lie
lye
my
nigh
phi
pi
pie
ply
pry
psi
rye
shy
sigh
sky
sly
spry
spy
sty
stye
thigh
thy
tie
try
vie
why
wry

(2)
ally
apply
awry
belie
bonsai
comply

*Rules for the lanterne are on p. 118.

deadeye
decry
defy
deny
descry
espy
good-by
imply
magpie
outcry
oxeye
rely
reply
supply
thereby
untie

(3)
alibi
alkali
amplify
butterfly
calcify
certify
clarify
classify
crucify
deify
dignify
dragonfly
fortify
glorify
goldeneye
justify
liquefy
lullaby
magnify
metrify
micrify

minify
misapply
modify
mollify
mortify
multiply
mystify
nigrify
notify
nullify
occupy
ossify
overlie
pacify
passerby
petrify
rectify
satisfy
signify
stulitify
terrify
testify
unify
verify
versify
vivify

IBE

bribe
gibe
jibe
scribe
stribe

(2)
ascribe
describe
imbibe

inscribe
prescribe
subscribe
transcribe

(3)
circumscribe
diatribe
superscribe

ICE

dice
ice
lice
mice
nice
price
rice
slice
spice
splice
thrice
vice
vise

(2)
advice
allspice
concise
device
entice
precise
suffice

(3)
paradise

ICH (see ITCH)

53

ICK

brick
chick
click
crick
flick
hick
kick
lick
nick
pick
prick
quick
rick
sic
sick
slick
snick
stick
thick
tic
tick
trick
wick

(2)
airsick
dipstick
diptych
distich
lipstick
nutpick
unstick

(3)
bailiwick
candlestick
candlewick
fiddlestick
heptastich
hexastich
monostich
overtrick
pentastich
tetrastich

ICT

strict

(2)
addict
afflict
conflict
constrict
convict
delict
depict
district
evict
inflict
predict
restrict

(3)
benedict
contradict
derelict
interdict
maledict

ID

bid
did
grid
hid
kid
lid
mid
quid
rid
skid
slid
squid

(2)
amid
forbid
nonskid
outdid
rebid
undid

(3)
katydid
overbid
underbid

IDE

bide
bride
chide
cried
died
dried
dyed
eyed
flied
fried
glide
guide
hide
lied
nide
pied
plied

pride
pried
ride
shied
side
sighed
slide
snide
spied
stride
tide
tied
tried
vied
wide

(2)
abide
allied
applied
aside
astride
belied
beside
bestride
betide
collide
confide
decide
decried
defied
deride
descried
divide
elide
espied
excide
implied
landslide

misguide
outride
outside
preside
provide
reside
subside
supplied
untried

(3)
deicide
fratricide
genocide
matricide
patricide
suicide
waterside

IFE

fife
knife
life
rife
strife
wife

(2)
alewife
jackknife
loosestrife
midwife
oldwife

(3)
afterlife

IFF

cliff

glyph
if
miff
riff
skiff
sniff
stiff
tiff
whiff
zif

IFT

drift
gift
lift
rift
shift
shrift

IG

big
brig
dig
fig
gig
grig
jig
pig
prig
rig
sprig
swig
trig
twig
whig
wig

(2)
bigwig
renege
shindig
unrig

(3)
perriwig
whirligig

IGHT (see ITE)

IKE

bike
dike
hike
like
mike
pike
shrike
spike
strike
trike
tyke

(2)
alike
dislike
unlike

ILD

build
gild
guild

ĪLD

child
mild

wild

ILE

aisle
bile
chyle
faille
file
guile
isle
lisle
mile
pile
rile
smile
stile
tile
vile
while
wile

(2)
anile
awhile
beguile
compile
defile
enisle
ensile
exile
resile
revile

(3)
crocodile
domicile
epistyle
infantile
microphyle

reconcile

ILL

bill
brill
chill
dill
drill
fill
gill
grill
grille
hill
ill
kill
mil
mill
nil
pill
quill
rill
shill
shrill
sill
skill
spill
squill
still
swill
thill
thrill
till
trill
twill
will

(2)
distill
downhill

freewill
instill
mandrill
molehill
nihil
quadrille
refill
until

　　(3)
chlorophyll
daffodil
escadrille
espadrille
mercantile
whippoorwill
winterkill

ILT

built
gilt
guilt
hilt
jilt
kilt
lilt
milt
quilt
silt
stilt
tilt
wilt

IM

brim
dim
grim
gym

him
hymn
limb
limn
prim
rim
scrim
shim
skim
slim
swim
trim
vim
whim

　　(2)
bedim

　　(3)
acronym
allonym
anonym
antonym
cryptonym
eponym
homonym
metonym
paronym
pseudonym
synonym
toponym

IME

chime
chyme
climb
clime
crime
dime

grime
lime
mime
prime
rhyme
rime
slime
thyme
time

　　(2)
begrime
enzyme
falltime
mealtime
meantime
springtime
sublime

　　(3)
aforetime
aftertime
maritime
overtime
pantomime
summertime
wintertime

IMP

blimp
crimp
gimp
guimpe
imp
limp
pimp
primp
scrimp

57

shrimp
skimp

IN

bin
chin
din
fin
grin
in
inn
kin
linn
pin
shin
sin
skin
spin
thin
tin
twin
win

(2)
begin
chagrin
kingpin
linchpin
moleskin
therein
within

(3)
candlepin
insulin
manikin
melanin
underpin

INCH

chinch
cinch
clinch
inch
finch
flinch
lynch
pinch
winch

IND

bind
blind
find
grind
hind
kind
mind
rind
wind

(2)
behind
mankind
purblind
unbind
unkind
unwind

(3)
humankind
mastermind
womankind

INE

bine
brine

chine
dine
fine
kine
line
mine
nine
pine
shine
shrine
sign
spine
spline
stein
swine
thine
tine
trine
twine
vine
whine
wine

(2)
align
assign
benign
canine
combine
condign
confine
consign
deadline
decline
define
design
divine
enshrine
entwine

58

incline
malign
opine
outshine
recline
refine
repine
resign
supine

(3)
anodyne
asinine
borderline
calcimine
columbine
concubine
countersign
eglantine
interline
intertwine
undermine
valentine

ING
bing
bring
cling
ding
fling
king
ming
ping
ring
sing
sling
spring
sting
string

swing
thing
ting
wing
wring

(2)
dayspring
lacewing
lapwing
latchstring
mainspring

(3)
a la king
anything
pigeonwing
sanderling
underling
underwing

INGE
binge
cringe
fringe
hinge
singe
tinge
twinge

(2)
astringe
constringe
impinge
infringe
syringe
unhinge

INK
blink
brink
chink
cinque
clink
dink
drink
fink
ink
kink
link
mink
pink
rink
shrink
sink
skink
slink
stink
swink
think
wink
zinc

(2)
bethink
hoodwink
unlink

(3)
bobolink
countersink
interlink

INT
dint
flint
glint

hint
lint
mint
print
quint
splint
sprint
squint
stint
tint

(2)
blueprint
imprint
misprint
reprint

(3)
aquatint
fingerprint
lithoprint
mezzotint
microprint
overprint
peppermint

IP

blip
chip
clip
dip
drip
flip
grip
grippe
gyp
hip
lip
nip

pip
quip
rip
scrip
ship
sip
skip
slip
snip
strip
tip
trip
whip
zip

(2)
airship
airstrip
equip
kingship
lordship
midship
outstrip
reship
transship
unrip

(3)
brinkmanship
horsemanship
internship
ladyship
ownership
scholarship
sportsmanship

IPE

gripe
pipe

ripe
snipe
stripe
swipe
tripe
type
wipe

(2)
jacksnipe
unripe

(3)
linotype
monotype

IR (see UR)
IRCH (see URCH)
IRD (see URD)

IRE

choir
dire
fire
hire
gyre
lyre
mire
pyre
quire
shire
sire
spire
squire
tire
wire

(2)
acquire

admire
afire
aspire
attire
backfire
bemire
conspire
desire
entire
enquire
esquire
expire
inquire
inspire
misfire
perspire
require
retire
rewire
suspire
transpire

IRK (see URK)
IRL (see URL)
IRM (see URM)
IRST (see URST)
IRT (see URT)
IRTH (see URTH)

ISH

cuish
dish
fish
pish
swish
whish
wish

(2)
beamish
brackish
flourish
languish
mawkish
nourish

ISK

bisque
brisk
disc
disk
fisc
frisk
risk
whisk

(3)
asterisk
basilisk
obelisk
odalisque
tamarisk

ISS

bis
bliss
cuisse
hiss
kiss
miss
sis
this

(2)
abyss
amiss
dismiss

remiss

(3)
cicatrice
cockatrice
dentifrice
licorice

IST

cist
cyst
fist
gist
grist
list
mist
tryst
twist
whist
wist
wrist

(2)
assist
consist
czarist
desist
enlist
entwist
exist
insist
jurist
linquist
lyrist
metrist
persist
resist
subsist
untwist

(3)
aorist
aphorist
atavist
atheist
catalyst
ceramist
classicist
coexist
colloquist
columnist
legalist
liturgist
lobbyist
lyricist
macrocyst
masochist
melodist
mesmerist
monarchist
moralist
narcissist
nepotist
oboist
oculist
optimist
plagiarist

IT

bit
bitt
brit
chit
fit
flit
frit
grit
hit

it
kit
knit
lit
mitt
nit
pit
quit
rit
sit
skit
slit
spit
split
sprit
tit
twit
whit
wit
writ

(2)
acquit
admit
befit
bowsprit
cesspit
cockpit
commit
conduit
demit
emit
half-wit
misfit
omit
outfit
outwit
permit
refit

remit
submit
transmit
unfit
unsplit

(3)
benefit
counterfeit
hypocrite
interknit
intromit
manumit
opposite
recommit

ITCH

bitch
ditch
fitch
flitch
hitch
itch
lich
miche
niche
pitch
quitch
rich
smitch
stitch
switch
twitch
which
witch

(2)
backstitch
bewitch

enrich
ostrich
restitch
unhitch

(3)
featherstitch

ITE

bight
bite
blight
bright
cite
dight
fight
flight
flite
fright
height
kite
knight
light
might
mite
night
plight
quite
right
rite
sight
site
sleight
slight
smite
spite
sprite
tight
trite

white
wite
wright
write

(2)
affright
alight
all right
aright
attrite
bedight
contrite
delight
despite
enflight
excite
ignite
incite
indict
indite
insight
invite
lucite
midnight
polite
recite
requite
rewrite
unite
upright

(3)
acolyte
anchorite
anthracite
appetite
blatherskite
copyright
eremite

erudite
expedite
Fahrenheit
granulite
laborite
neophyte
oversight
parasite
proselyte
recondite
satellite
sybarite
watertight

ITH

kith
myth
pith
smith
with
withe

(2)
goldsmith
locksmith

(3)
acrolith
batholith
coppersmith
eolith
ironsmith
megalith
monolith
neolith
silversmith
xenolith

ĪTH

blithe

scythe
tithe
writhe

ĪVE

chive
dive
drive
five
gyve
jive
live
rive
scrive
shive
shrive
skive
strive
thrive
wive

(2)
alive
arrive
connive
contrive
deprive
derive
ogive
revive
survive

IVE

give
live
sieve

(2)
forgive

misgive
outlive

IX

fix
mix
nix
six

(2)
admix
affix
commix
matrix
optics
prefix
prolix
remix
transfix

(3)
antefix
appendix
cicatrix
crucifix
intermix
melodics

IZE

ayes
buys
cries
dies
drys
dyes
eyes
flys
frys
guise

guys
hies
highs
lies
mise
pies
plies
prize
prys
rise
sighs
size
skies
stys
styes
thighs
ties
tries
whys
wise

(2)
advise
baptize
capsize
comprise
demise
despise
disguise
incise
likewise

(3)
advertise
authorize
burglarize
circumcise
compromise
dramatize
enterprise

improvise
merchandise
mesmerize
otherwise
realize
rhapsodize
satirize
sterilize
vitalize
vocalize

IBBLE

(2)
dibble
dribble
fribble
gribble
nibble
quibble
scribble
sibyl

IBLE

(3)
feasible
flexible
forcible
horrible
legible
plausible
possible
sensible
tangible
terrible
vincible
visible

(4)
convincible
divisible
illegible
impassible
implausible
invincible
ostensible
perceptible
pervertible
reducible
remissible
repressible
responsible
reversible
seducible
submergible
suggestible
susceptible
transfusible
transmissible

ICIOUS

(2)
vicious

(3)
capricious
delicious
fictitious
judicious
pernicious
propitious
seditious

(4)
avaricious
meretricious
repetitious

superstitious

ICIT

(2)
licit

(3)
deficit
explicit
illicit
implicit
solicit

ICITY

(4)
complicity
duplicity
felicity
mendicity
publicity
simplicity
tonicity
toxicity

ICKER

(2)
bicker
dicker
flicker
liquor
picker
quicker
sicker
slicker
snicker
sticker
ticker
vicar

wicker

(3)
frolicker
ragpicker
trafficker

ICKLE

(2)
fickle
nickel
pickle
sickle
stickle
strickle
tickle
trickle

(3)
icicle
radical
radicle
reticle
tunicle
vehicle
ventricle
versicle
vericle

ICTION

(2)
diction
fiction
friction

(3)
constriction

conviction
depiction
indiction
infliction
restriction
suffixion
transfixion

(4)
contradiction
crucifixion
dereliction
jurisdiction
malediction
valediction

IDDEN

(2)
bidden
hidden
ridden

(3)
bedridden
unbidden

IDDLE

(2)
fiddle
griddle
middle
piddle
riddle
twiddle

IDER

(2)
cider

glider
rider
spider
wider

(3)
outrider
outsider

IDITY

(4)
frigidity
humidity
liquidity
morbidity
placidity
rabidity
solidity
stolidity
stupidity
timidity
torpidity
tumidity
turgidity
validity
vapidity

IDLE

(2)
bridal
bridle
idle
idol
idyl
seidel
sidle
tidal

(4)
genocidal
herbicidal
homicidal
matricidal
paracidal
patricidal
suicidal

IER

(2)
brier
buyer
crier
drier
dyer
flyer
fryer
higher
liar
nigher
plier
prior
pryer
shier
shyer
slyer
spryer

(3)
complier
defier

(4)
mollifier
multiplier
prophesier
qualifier
ratifier

rectifier
signifier
simplifier
testifier
typifier
unifier

IETY

(3)
piety

(4)
anxiety
impiety
propriety
satiety
sobriety
society
ubiety
variety

IFTER

(2)
drifter
grifter
lifter
sifter
snifter
swifter

IGGER

(2)
bigger
chigger
digger
jigger
rigger

rigor
snigger
swigger
trigger
vigor

(3)
gravedigger
outrigger

IGGLE

(2)
giggle
higgle
jiggle
niggle
sniggle
wiggle
wriggle

ILDER

(2)
builder
gilder

(3)
bewilder

ĪLDER

milder
wilder

ILITY

(4)
ability
civility
docility

facility
fertility
fragility
futility
hostility
humility
mobility
nobility
scurrility
senility
servility
stability
tranquillity
utility
virility

ILLER

(2)
driller
filler
killer
miller
pillar
thriller
tiller

ILLION

(2)
billion
jillion
million
trillion
zillion

(3)
cotillion
decillion
modillion

nonillion
octillion
pavillion
quadrillion
quintillion
septillion
sextillion
tourbillion
vermillion

ILLY

(2)
billy
chilly
filly
frilly
hilly
lily
silly

(4)
willy-nilly

IMBLE

(2)
cymbal
nimble
symbol
thimble
timbal
timbale
wimble

IMMER

(2)
crimmer
dimmer
glimmer

grimmer
primer
shimmer
simmer
skimmer
slimmer
swimmer
trimmer

IMPLE

(2)
crimple
dimple
pimple
simple
wimple

ĪNDER

(2)
binder
blinder
finder
grinder
hinder
minder
winder

(3)
highbinder
pathfinder
reminder
sidewinder

INDER

cinder
hinder
tinder

INDLE

(2)
bindle
brindle
dindle
dwindle
kindle
spindle
swindle

INER

(2)
diner
finer
liner
miner
minor
shiner
signer
whiner

(3)
headliner
moonshiner

INGER

(2)
finger
linger
ringer
singer
slinger
springer
stinger
stringer
wringer

(3)
humdinger
malinger

INGLE

(2)
dingle
jingle
mingle
shingle
single
tingle
swingle

INION

(2)
minion
pinion

(3)
dominion
opinion

INIT

(2)
linnet
minute
rennet
spinet

INITY

(3)
trinity

(4)
devinity
felinity
infinity

salinity
vicinity
virginity

(5)
femininity

INJER

(2)
cringer
injure
ginger
singer

(3)
impinger
peringer

INKER

(2)
blinker
clinker
sinker
stinker
tinker
winker

INKLE

(2)
inkle
crinkle
sprinkle
tinkle
twinkle
winkle
wrinkle

(3)
besprinkle

(4)
periwinkle

INNER

(2)
dinner
inner
sinner
skinner
spinner
thinner
tinner
winner

(3)
beginner

IPPER

(2)
chipper
clipper
dipper
flipper
gripper
kipper
nipper
ripper
shipper
sipper
skipper
slipper
stripper
tipper
tripper
whipper
zipper

IPPLE

(2)
cripple
nipple
ripple
stipple
tipple

IPTION

(3)
description
inscription
prescription
proscription
subscription
transcription

(4)
superscription

ISER

(2)
geyser
kaiser
miser
riser
wiser

(3)
advisor
baptizer
incisor

(4)
advertiser
compromiser
equalizer
fertilizer
mesmerizer

vocalizer
supervisor

ISION

(2)
scission
vision

(3)
decision
derision
devision
concision
incision
misprision
precision
prevision
provision
revision

(4)
circumcision
improvision
supervision

ISSION

(2)
fission
mission

(3)
admission
attrition
commission
condition
contrition
emission
fruition
magician

monition
mortician
musician
nutrition
omission
partition
patrician
patrition
perdition
permission
petition
physician
position
remission
rendition
sedition
submission
suspicion
tactician
technician
tradition
transition
transmission
vendition
volition

ISSLE

(2)
bristle
gristle
missal
missel
missile
scissile
sisal
thistle
whistle

(3)
epistle

ISTER

(2)
blister
glister
lister
mister
sister
twister

ISTIC

(2)
cystic
mystic

(3)
juristic
logistic
monistic
papistic
patristic
simplistic
sophistic
statistic
stylistic
theistic

ITER

(2)
blighter
brighter
fighter
lighter
miter
niter
tighter

writer

(3)
lamplighter
re-writer

(4)
copywriter
expediter
underwriter

ITHER

(2)
dither
hither
slither
thither
wither
whither

ITIC

(2)
critic

(3)
enclitic
graphitic
mephitic
nephritic
phrenitic
pleuritic
politic
proclitic

(4)
analytic
eremitic
paralytic
parasitic
photolytic

ITTEN

(2)
bitten
kitten
mitten
smitten
written

ITTER

(2)
bitter
critter
fitter
flitter
fritter
glitter
hitter
jitter
knitter
litter
quitter
sitter
skitter
slitter
spitter
splitter
titter
twitter

(3)
atwitter
embitter
hairsplitter
remittor
transmitter

ITTLE

(2)
brittle
little
skittle
victual
whittle

(3)
acquittal

ITTY

(2)
city
ditty
gritty
kitty
pity
pretty
witty

ĪVER

(2)
diver
fiver
skiver
stiver

(3)
survivor

IVER

(2)
giver
liver
quiver
river
shiver

sliver

(3)
deliver
lawgiver

IZZARD

(2)
blizzard
gizzard
izzard
lizard
vizard
wizard

IZZLE

(2)
drizzle
fizzle
frizzle
grizzle
sizzle
swizzle

O

beau
blow
bow
crow
do
doe
dough
eau

foe
floe
flow
fro
froe
frow
glow
go
grow
ho
hoe
know
low
mot
mow
no
noh
oh
owe
roe
row
sew
show
sloe
slow
snow
so
sow
stow
strow
though
throe
throw
toe
tow
trop
trow
whoa
woe

(2)
aglow
ago
although
bandeau
below
bestow
bestrow
bistro
chapeau
chateau
checkrow
cockcrow
crossbow
depot
ditto
embow
escrow
forego
foreknow
foreshow
jabot
jambeau
jingo
jumbo
junco
keno
largo
lasso
lento
limbo
lingo
lobo
loco
longbow
lotto
maestro
maillot
mallow

mango
manteau
marrow
meadow
mellow
memo
mezzo
milo
motto
mucro
mungo
niello
oboe
outgrow
oxbow
plateau
rondeau
rondo
sabot
tableau
tonneau
tricot
unsew

(3)
adagio
afterglow
agio
alamo
allegro
alpenglow
amino
apropos
arpeggio
bungalow
calico
cameo
counterblow
domino

do-si-do
dynamo
entrepot
escargot
fabliau
folio
fricandeau
fubelow
gigolo
indigo
inferno
libido
libretto
magnito
memento
merino
mikado
mistletoe
morello
mosquito
mulatto
octavo
oleo
olio
overblow
overflow
overgrow
overthrow
paramo
staccato
tallyho
undergo
undertow

(4)
innuendo
intermezzo
majordomo
manifesto

OACH

broach
brooch
coach
loach
poach
roach

(2)
abroach
approach
caroche
cockroach
encroach
reproach

OAD (see ODE)
OAK (see OKE)
OAL (see OLE)
OAM (see OME)
OAN (see OWN)
OAR (see ORE)
OAST (see OST)
OAT (see OTE)

OB

bob
blob
cob
fob
gob
glob
hob
job
knob
lob
mob
nob

rob
sob
slob
snob
throb

(2)
corncob
doorknob
hobnob
nabob

OBE

globe
lobe
probe
robe

(2)
conglobe
disrobe
enrobe
microbe
unrobe

OCK

bock
bloc
block
clock
cock
crock
dock
floc
flock
frock
hock
jock
knock

lock
mock
pock
roc
rock
shock
smock
sock
stock

(2)
deadlock
defrock
diestock
lovelock
matchlock
o'clock
unfrock
unlock

(3)
alpenstock
fetterlock
hollyhock
interlock
laughingstock
overstock
poppycock
shuttlecock
weathercock

OD

clod
cod
god
hod
mod
nod
odd

plod
pod
prod
rod
scrod
shod
sod
trod

(3)
demigod
goldenrod
hexapod
isopod
megapod
octopod
pseudopod

ODE

bode
code
goad
load
lode
mode
node
ode
road
rode
toad
yodh

(2)
abode
anode
commode
corrode
decode
displode

epode
erode
explode
implode
reload
unload

(3)
a la mode
discommode
episode
internode
monopode
nematode
overload
palinode
pigeontoed

OFT

croft
loft
oft
soft

(2)
aloft

OG

bog
clog
cog
dog
flog
fog
frog
grog
hog
jog

log
nog
slog
smog
tog

(3)
analog
apologue
catalogue
demagogue
dialogue
epilogue
golliwog
monologue
pettifog
polliwog
synagogue

ŌG

brogue
rogue
vogue

(2)
collogue
prorogue

(3)
disembogue

OIL

boil
broil
coil
foil
moil
noil
oil

roil
soil
spoil
toil
voile

(2)
despoil
embroil
gargoyle
recoil
uncoil

OIN

coin
groin
join
loin
quoin

(2)
adjoin
conjoin
disjoin
enjoin
purloin
recoin
rejoin
subjoin

(3)
tenderloin

OINT

joint
point

(2)
anoint
appoint

conjoint
disjoint
outpoint
unjoint

(3)
counterpoint
disappoint

OISE

boys
cloys
hoise
joys
noise
poise
toys

(3)
counterpoise
equipoise

OIST

foist
hoist
joist
moist
voiced

(2)
invoiced
rejoiced

OKE

bloke
broke
choke
cloak

coke
croak
folk
joke
oak
poke
soak
smoke
spoke
stoke
stroke
woke
yoke
yolk

(2)
awoke
baroque
convoke
evoke
invoke
menfolk
provoke
restoke
revoke

(3)
counterstroke
gentlefolk
womenfolk

OLD

bold
bowled
cold
fold
gold
hold
mold

old
scold
sold
told

(2)
behold
enfold
enrolled
remold
unfold
unmold
untold
uphold
withhold

(3)
centerfold
interfold
manifold
marigold
multifold
overbold

OLE

bole
boll
bowl
coal
cole
dole
droll
foal
goal
hole
knoll
mole
pole
poll

role
roll
scroll
shoal
skoal
sol
sole
soul
stole
stroll
toll
troll
whole

(2)
cajole
charcoal
condole
console
control
enroll
ensoul
extol
insole
logroll
manhole
parole
patrol
resole
unroll

(3)
aureole
buttonhole
cabriole
camisole
casserole
decontrol

77

escarole
oriole
oversoul
pigeonhole
rigmarole

OLT

bolt
colt
dolt
jolt
molt
smolt
volt

(2)
revolt
unbolt

(3)
demivolt
millivolt
thunderbolt

OLVE

solve

(2)
absolve
convolve
dissolve
involve
resolve
revolve

(3)
circumvolve
intervolve

OME

brome
chrome
comb
dome
foam
gnome
home
loam
ohm
roam
tome

(2)
airdrome
coxcomb

(3)
acrodome
astrodome
catacomb
chromosome
currycomb
hippodrome
honeycomb
metronome
monochrome
palindrome
peristome
polychrome
styrofoam

ON

con
don

(2)
anon
begone

bygone
chiffon
crouton
micron
moron
mouton
orlon
thereon
whereon

(3)
antiphon
carillon
colophon
cyclotron
decagon
demijohn
epsilon
etymon
heptagon
hexagon
marathon
mastadon
octagon
omicron
pantheon
papillon
paragon
pentagon
polygon
positron
tetragon
thereupon
whereupon
woebegon

(4)
automaton

78

OND

blond
blonde
bond
fond
frond
pond

(2)
abscond
beyond
despond
millpond
respond

(3)
correspond
demimonde
vagabond

ONG

bong
cong
dong
gong
long
prong
song
strong
thong
throng
tong
wrong

(2)
along
belong
dingdong
diphthong

erelong
lifelong
livelong
oblong
oolong
pingpong
prolong
sarong

(3)
billabong
cradlesong
evensong
monophthong
scuppernong

ONT (see UNT)

OO*
* indicates that
many words may
be pronounced
with either OO
or long U sounds

blew
blue
boo
brew
chew
clew
clue
coo
coup
crew
dew
do
drew
due

flew
flue
glue
gnu
grew
knew
lieu
loo
moo
moue
mu
new
nu
pooh
pugh
roux
rue
screw
shoe
shoo
shrew
slew
slough
slue
sou
stew
strew
sue
threw
through
to
too
true
two
who
woo
yew
you
zoo

(2)
accrue
adieu
ado
anew
bamboo
bedew
canoe
construe
corkscrew
cuckoo
endue
ensue
eschew
fondue
indue
into
issue
jackscrew
mildew
milieu
outgrew
perdue
pursue
ragout
renew
shampoo
subdue
taboo
undo
undue
unglue
unscrew
unto
untrue
virtue
withdrew

(3)
avenue
ballyhoo
caribou
cockatoo
honeydew
impromptu
ingenue
jujitsu
kangaroo
misconstrue
overdo
overdue
overshoe
parvenu
peekaboo
rendezvous
retinue
revenue

OOD*

brood
crude
dude
food
lewd
mood
nude
prude
rood
rude
shrewd
snood
sued

(2)
allude
collude
conclude
delude
denude
detrude
endued
elude
extrude
exude
include
intrude
obtrude
occlude
preclude
protrude

(3)
altitude
amplitude
aptitude
attitude
interlude

OOL

cool
drool
fool
ghoul
pool
rule
school
spool
stool
tool
tulle

(2)
befool
cesspool
lunule
misrule
mutule
retool

OOM*

boom
bloom
broom
brume
doom
flume
gloom
groom
loom
plume
rheum
room
tomb
whom
womb
zoom

(2)
abloom
assume
checkroom
consume
costume
deplume
entomb
mushroom
pantoum
presume
resume

(3)
anteroom
disentomb
elbowroom
nom de plume

OON*

boon

coon
croon
dune
goon
loon
lune
moon
noon
prune
rune
soon
spoon
strewn
swoon
tune

(2)
attune
baboon
balloon
bassoon
bestrewn
bridoon
buffoon
cartoon
cocoon
doubloon
dragoon
festoon
harpoon
jejune
lagoon
lampoon
maroon
monsoon
patroon
platoon
poltroon
pontoon
quadroon

saloon
spittoon
teaspoon
tycoon
typhoon

(3)
afternoon
demilune
honeymoon
macaroon
octoroon
opportune
pantaloon
picaroon
puppetoon
saskatoon
tablespoon

OOP*

coop
croup
dupe
drupe
goop
group
hoop
loop
poop
roup
scoop
sloop
snoop
soup
stoop
stoup
stupe
swoop
troop

troupe
whoop

(2)
recoup
regroup

OOR

boor
dour
lure
moor
poor
stour
tour
your

(2)
abjure
adjure
allure
assure
objure
unmoor

OOSE*

deuce
goose
juice
loose
luce
moose
mousse
noose
nous
puce
sluice
spruce
truce

use

(2)
abstruse
adduce
caboose
ceruse
conduce
deduce
educe
induce
obtuse
mongoose
papoose
produce
recluse
reduce
seduce
vamoose

(3)
calaboose
goldengoose
introduce
reproduce

OOT*

boot
bruit
brute
coot
flute
fruit
hoot
jute
loot
lute
moot
newt

root
route
scoot
snoot
suit
toot

(2)
astute
dilute
disroot
enroot
enroute
lawsuit
offshoot
outshoot
pursuit
recruit
salute
uproot
volute

(3)
absolute
arrowroot
bandicoot
bitterroot
constitute
evolute
feverroot
marabout
obvolute
orrisroot
overshoot
parachute

OOTH

booth
couth

sleuth
sooth
tooth
truth
youth

(2)
dogtooth
forsooth
vermouth
uncouth
untruth

OOVE

groove
hoove
move
prove

(2)
approve
behoove
commove
disprove
improve
regroove
remove
reprove

(3)
countermove
disapprove
microgroove

OOZE*

booze
bruise
choose
cruise

cruse
fuse
lose
ooze
ruse
snooze
thews
whose

(2)
abuse
accuse
amuse
contuse
enthuse
peruse

OP

bop
chop
cop
crop
drop
fop
flop
hop
lop
mop
pop
prop
shop
slop
sop
stop
strop
swap
top
whop
wop

(2)
backdrop
backstop
bellhop
carhop
dewdrop
doorstop
estop
maintop
milksop
tiptop
unstop

(3)
intercrop
lollipop

OPE

cope
dope
grope
hope
lope
mope
pope
rope
scope
slope
soap
stope
taupe
trope

(2)
aslope
dragrope
elope

(3)
aeroscope

altiscope
antelope
cantaloupe
chronoscope
envelope
gyroscope
heliotrope
hydroscope
interlope
isotope
kinescope
microscope
misanthrope
pantoscope
periscope
telescope

ORD

board
bored
chord
chored
cord
fjord
gourd
hoard
horde
lord
sward
sword
toward
ward
whored

(2)
aboard
accord
afford
discord

inboard
landlord
matchboard
milord
outboard
record
reward

(3)
clavicord
disaccord
monochord
octacord
overlord

ORE

boar
bore
chore
core
corps
door
floor
fore
four
gore
hoar
lore
more
oar
ore
pore
pour
roar
score
shore
snore
soar
sore

spore
store
swore
tore
whore
wore
yore

(2)
adore
afore
ashore
before
decor
deplore
downpour
explore
galore
ignore
implore
indoor
inpour
inshore
outpour
outsoar
restore
uproar

(3)
battledore
carnivore
commodore
cuspidore
evermore
furthermore
herbivore
humidor
matador
microspore
nevermore

overscore
picador
pinafore
pompadour
semaphore
sophomore
stevedore
sycamore
troubadour
underscore
zygospore

ORM

corm
dorm
form
norm
storm
swarm
warm

(2)

conform
deforn
inform
lukewarm
perform
reform
transform

(3)

cruciform
deiform
multiform
thunderstorm
uniform

ÔRN or ŌRN

born
borne
bourne
corn
horn
lorn
morn
mourn
scorn
shorn
sworn
thorn
warn
worn

(2)

adorn
blackthorn
careworn
dehorn
foresworn
forewarn
inborn
inkhorn
lovelorn
reborn
suborn
unborn
unworn
uptorn

(3)

alpenhorn
barleycorn
clavicorn
peppercorn
unicorn
waterworn
weatherworn

winterbourne

ÔRSE

coarse
course
force
gorse
horse
source

(2)

concourse
deforce
discourse
divorce
endorse
extrorse
introrse
premorse
remorse
unhorse

(3)

hobbyhorse
intercourse

ORT

bort
court
fort
forte
mort
ort
port
quart
short
snort
sport
thwart

torte

(2)
abort
aport
assort
athwart
cavort
cohort
comport
consort
contort
deport
disport
distort
escort
extort
intort
report
resort
retort
support
transport

OSE

close
dose
gross

(2)
cirrose
dextrose
engross
jocose
morose
osmose
verbose

(3)
adipose

ariose
bellicose
comatose
diagnose
grandiose
hematose
otiose
overdose
varicose

OSS

boss
cross
dross
foss
floss
gloss
loss
moss

(2)
across
emboss
lacrosse

(3)
albatross
intercross

OST

boast
coast
dosed
ghost
host
most
oast
post
roast

toast

(2)
almost
compost
impost
midmost
outmost
outpost
riposte

(3)
aftermost
furthermost
hithermost
innermost
lattermost
lowermost
nethermost
outermost
uppermost
uttermost

OST

cost
frost
lost

(2)
accost
defrost
exhaust

OT

blot
clot
cot
dot

got
grot
hot
jot
knot
lot
not
plot
pot
rot
scot
shot
slot
spot
sot
tot
trot

(2)
allot
begot
besot
forgot
jackpot
mascot
unknot

(3)
apricot
bergamot
counterplot
flowerpot
monkeypot
overshot
polyglot

OTCH

blotch
botch

crotch
nautch
notch
scotch
splotch

OTE

bloat
boat
coat
cote
dote
float
gloat
goat
moat
mote
note
oat
quote
rote
shoat
smote
stoat
throat
tote
troat
vote
wrote

(2)
afloat
capote
compote
connote
demote
denote
devote
devecote

emote
misquote
promote
remote
u-boat
unquote

(3)
anecdote
antidote
cockleboat
creosote
ferryboat
overcoat
petticoat
redingote
table d'hote
undercoat
yellowthroat

OTH

broth
cloth
froth
moth
sloth
troth
wroth

ŌTH

both
growth
oath
quoth

(2)
outgrowth
upgrowth

OUD

cloud
crowd
loud
proud
shroud

(2)
aloud
becloud
unshroud

(3)
overcloud
overloud
thundercloud

OUGH (see UFF)

OUGHT

aught
bought
brought
caught
fought
fraught
naught
nought
ought
sought
taught
taut
thought
wrought

(2)
besought
distraught
onslaught

unsought
untaught

(3)
aeronaut
afterthought
argonaut
astronaut
cosmonaut
overwrought

OUL (see OWL)

OUNCE

bounce
flounce
frounce
jounce
ounce
pounce
trounce

(2
announce
denounce
enounce
pronounce
renounce

OUND

bound
found
ground
hound
mound
pound
round
sound
wound

(2)
abound
aground
around
astound
compound
confound
expound
impound
profound
rebound
redound
resound
surround
unsound
unwound

OUNT

count
fount
mount

(2)
account
amount
demount
discount
dismount
miscount
recount
remount
surmount

(3)
catamount
paramount

OUR

dour

flour
hour
our
scour
sour

(2)
devour

OUSE

douse
grouse
house
louse
mouse
souse
spouse

(2)
alehouse
almshouse
courthouse
delouse
dormouse
lighthouse
madhouse

(3)
bawdyhouse
pilothouse

OUT

bout
clout
doubt
drought
flout
gout
grout

knout
lout
out
pout
rout
scout
shout
snout
spout
sprout
stout
tout
trout

(2)
about
blackout
devout
layout
lookout
without

(3)
gadabout
hereabout
knockabout
roundabout
roustabout
runabout
thereabout
waterspout
whirlabout

OUZ

blouse
boughs
bows
browse
chouse

cows
dowse
drowse
grouse
house
mows
plows
prows
rouse
scows
vows
wows

(2)
allows
arouse
avows
carouse
endows
espouse
unhouse

OVE

cove
clove
dove
drove
grove
hove
mauve
rove
shrove
stove
strove
trove
wove

OVE (see UV)

OW

bough
bow
brow
chow
cow
frow
how
mow
plow
pow
prow
row
scow
sow
thou
vow

(2)
allow
avow
chowchow
endow
kowtow
meow
powwow

OWL

cowl
foul
fowl
howl
jowl
owl

ŌWN

blown
bone
clone
cone
drone
flown
groan
grown
hone
known
loan
lone
moan
mown
own
phone
pone
prone
roan
scone
sewn
shone
shown
sown
stone
throne
thrown
tone
zone

(2)
alone
atone
bemoan
capstone
cologne
condone
copestone
cyclone
depone
dethrone
disown
impone
intone
keystone
lodestone
milestone
millstone
moonstone
mudstone
outgrown
ozone
postpone
resewn
resown
unknown
unmown
unsown

OWN

brown
clown
crown
drown
frown
gown
noun
town

(2)
discrown
renown
uncrown
uptown

OX

box
cox
fox
lox
ox
phlox
pox

sox
vox

(2)
boondocks
cowpox
mailbox
matchbox

(3)
chatterbox
equinox
goldilocks
orthodox
paradox
pepperbox
tinderbox

OY

boy
coy
cloy
foy
hoy
joy
ploy
soy
troy

(2)
ahoy
alloy
bellboy
decoy
deploy
destroy
doughboy
employ
enjoy
linkboy
octroi

teapoy
travois
viceroy

(3)
carboloy
corduroy
hoi polloi
maccaboy
misemploy
overjoy
paperboy
permalloy
redeploy
saveloy

OZE

bows
chose
close
clothes
crows
doze
flows
froes
froze
glows
goes
grows
hoes
hose
knows
lows
mows
nose
pose
prose
rows
sews
sows

stows
strows
those
throes
throws
toes
tows
woes

(2)
appose
arose
bestows
compose
disclose
enclose
expose
oppose
repose
suppose
transpose

OBBLE

(2)
cobble
gobble
hobble
wobble

OBBY

(2)
bobby
hobby
knobby
lobby
nobby

OCKER

(2)
cocker

docker
knocker
locker
rocker
shocker
soccer

(3)
footlocker

ODDER

(2)
dodder
fodder
plodder
prodder
solder

ODDLE

(2)
coddle
model
noddle
toddle

(4)
mollycoddle

ODGER

(2)
codger
dodger
lodger
roger

OGGLE

(2)
boggle

goggle
joggle
toggle

(3)
boondoggle
hornswoggle

OILER

(2)
boiler
broiler
oiler
toiler

OKEN

(2)
broken
oaken
spoken
token

(3)
heartbroken
housebroken
outspoken

OKER

(2)
broker
choker
croaker
joker
poker
smoker
stoker

(3)
stockbroker

(4)
mediocre

OLDEN

(2)
golden
olden

(3)
beholden
embolden

OLDER

(2)
bolder
boulder
colder
folder
holder
molder
older
smolder

(3)
potholder
stockholder

(4)
manifolder

OLER

(2)
bowler
dolor
molar
polar
roller
solar
stroller

(3)
charcoaler
comptroller
logroller
patroller

OLLER

(2)
choler
collar
dollar
scholar

OLLOW

(2)
follow
hollow
swallow
wallow

OLLY

(2)
collie
colly
dolly
folly
golly
holly
jolly
molly
polly
volley

(3)
loblolly

(4)
melancholy

OLOGY

(4)
apology
chronology
doxology
geology
graphology
histology
homology
hymnology
hypnology
ichnology
limnology
micrology
misology
monology
mythology
necrology
neology
ontology
pathology
pedology
philology
phonology
phrenology
psychology
sarcology
scatology
sexology
symbology
technology
theology
topology
trapology

typology
zoology
zymology

ONIC

(2)
chronic
phonic
sonic
tonic

(3)
atonic
bubonic
demonic
euphonic
gnomonic
harmonic
hedonic
hydronic
iconic
ionic
ironic
ketonic
laconic
mnemonic
moronic
platonic
pneumonic
sardonic
sermonic
subsonic
subtonic
symphonic
synchronic
transsonic
typhonic

OOMER

(2)
bloomer
roomer
rumor
tumor

(3)
consumer

OONER

(2)
crooner
lunar
pruner
schooner
sooner
spooner
tuner

(4)
honeymooner
interlunar

OOPER

(2)
cooper
hooper
looper
super
trouper
whooper

OOTER

(2)
neuter
scooter
shooter

suitor

OPIC

(2)
topic
tropic

(4)
geotropic
gyroscopic
hydroscopic
microscopic
misanthropic
periscopic
philanthropic
phototropic
telescopic

OPPER

(2)
copper
cropper
dropper
hopper
lopper
mopper
popper
proper
shopper
stopper
topper

OPPY

(2)
choppy
copy
floppy
poppy

sloppy

(3)
jalopy

ORITY

(4)
authority
majority
minority
priority
seniority
sonority
sorority

ORMER

(2)
dormer
former
swarmer
warmer

(3)
barnstormer
informer
performer
reformer

ORROW

(2)
borrow
morrow
sorrow

(3)
tomorrow

ORY

(2)
dory
glory
hoary
lory
story
tory

(4)
dormitory
hortatory
laudatory
lavatory
mandatory
minatory
monitory
moratory
offertory
predatory
prefatory
prelusory
promissory
promontory
pulsatory
punitory
purgatory
repertory
rotatory
saltatory
sanatory
signatory
statutory
transitory
vibratory

OSION

(3)
corrosion
erosion
exosion
explosion

OSIS

(2)
gnosis
ptosis

(3)
fibrosis
hypnosis
lordosis
morphosis
narcosis
nephrosis
necrosis
osmosis
psychosis
sclerosis
sycosis

OSITY

(4)
monstrosity
plumosity
pomposity
serosity
velocity
verbosity

(5)
animosity
curiosity
generosity
luminosity
preciosity
virtuosity

OSTER

(2)
coaster
poster
roaster
toaster

OSURE

(2)
closure

(3)
composure
disclosure
disposure
enclosure
explosure
foreclosure
inclosure

OSY

(2)
cozy
nosy
posey
rosy

OTHER (see UTHER)

OTIC

(3)
despotic
erotic
exotic
hypnotic
narcotic
neurotic
osmotic

psychotic

(4)
idiotic
patriotic
symbiotic

OTION

(2)
lotion
motion
notion
ocean
potion

(3)
demotion
devotion
promotion

(4)
locomotion

OTTER

(2)
blotter
cotter
hotter
knotter
plotter
potter
rotter
spotter
totter
trotter

OTTLE

(2)
bottle

mottle
pottle
throttle

OUNDER

(2)
bounder
flounder
founder
pounder
rounder
sounder

OVER

(2)
clover
over
plover
rover
stover
trover

(3)
crossover
moreover
stopover
turnover
walkover

OVER (see UVER)

OWEL

(2)
bowel
dowel
rowel
towel

trowel
vowel

(3)
avowal

(4)
disavowal
disembowel
semivowel

OWER

(2)
bower
cower
dower
flower
glower
plower
power
shower
tower

(3)
dayflower
deflower
embower
firepower
frostflower
mistflower
moonflower
pasqueflower
safflower
sunflower
wallflower

(4)
cauliflower
overpower

96

ŌWER

(2)
blower
crower
grower
knower
lower
mower
ower
rower
sower
slower
snower
stower
strower
thrower

(3)
bestower
safeblower
wayshower
winegrower
winnower
woolgrower

. . . words
collided
stark as truth
saying something
something soaring
this is IT
I thought
beautiful
excruciating
SOMETHING.

—Marjorie Culver
(from her book,
Wintergreen)

U

cue
ewe
few
hew
hue
mew
pew
queue
skew
spew
view
yew
you

(2)
curfew
debut
imbue
menu
miscue
nephew
preview
prevue
purview
review

(3)
barbecue
continue
curlicue
feverfew
interview
retinue
teleview

UB

chub
club

cub
drub
dub
grub
hub
nub
pub
rub
scrub
shrub
slub
snub
stub
tub

UCE (see OOSE)
UCH (see UTCH)

UCT

duct

(2)
abduct
conduct
construct
deduct
eruct
induct
instruct
obstruct
reluct
subduct

U̇D

could
good
hood
should

stood
wood
would

(2)
manhood
withstood

(3)
livelihood
maidenhood
neighborhood
widowhood

UD

blood
bud
crud
cud
dud
flood
mud
spud
stud
thud

UDE*
cued
feud
hewed
hued
mewed
queued
stewed
sued
viewed

(2)
delude
endued

ensued
étude
exude
imbued
intrude
pursued
renewed
reviewed
subdued
transude

(3)
desuetude
finitude
fortitude
gratitude
interlude
lassitude
latitude
longitude
magnitude
multitude
platitude
plenitude
quietude
rectitude
servitude

(4)
ineptitude
definitude

UDGE

budge
drudge
fudge
grudge
judge
nudge

sludge
smudge
trudge

(2)
adjudge
begrudge
misjudge
prejudge

UFF

bluff
buff
clough
cuff
duff
fluff
gruff
guff
huff
muff
puff
rough
ruff
scuff
slough
snuff
sough
stuff
tough

(2)
crossruff
enough
rebuff
unrough

UG

bug

drug
dug
hug
jug
lug
mug
plug
pug
shrug
slug
smug
snug
tug

(3)
jitterbug
ladybug
litterbug
scatterrug
tumblebug

UK

book
brook
cook
crook
hook
look
nook
rook
shook
stook
took
tuque

(2)
forsook
mistook
mainsook

notebook
partook
unhook

(3)
inglenook
overlook

UKE*

duke
fluke
kook
puke
spook
uke

(2)
peruke
rebuke

(3)
Pentateuch

ULE

mewl
mule
pule
ule
yule

(2)
labule
ligule
macule
module
nodule
ovule

(3)
majuscule

minuscule
molecule
monticule
reticule
vestibule

ULL

cull
dull
gull
hull
lull
mull
null
scull
skull

(2)
annul
numskull

ULSE

pulse

(2)
convulse
impulse
repulse
revulse

ULT

cult

(2)
adult
consult
exult
insult
occult

result

(3)
catapult
difficult

UM

bum
chum
come
crumb
drum
dumb
from
glum
gum
hum
mum
numb
plum
plumb
rum
scum
slum
some
strum
sum
swum
thumb

(2)
become
benumb
income
succumb

(3)
kettledrum
maximum
minimum

overcome
sugarplum

UME*

fume
spume

(2)
assume
consume
exhume
inhume
legume
perfume

UMP

bump
chump
clump
crump
dump
frump
grump
hump
jump
lump
mump
plump
pump
rump
slump
stump
sump
trump

UN

bun
done

dun
fun
gun
hun
none
nun
one
pun
run
shun
son
spun
stun
sun
ton
won

(2)
begun
millrun
someone
undone

(3)
anyone
megaton

UNCH

bunch
brunch
crunch
hunch
lunch
munch
punch
scrunch

UND

bund

100

dunned
fund
gunned
punned
shunned
stunned
sunned

(2)
obtund
refund
rotund

(3)
cummerbund
moribund
orotund
rubicund

UNE

hewn

(2)
commune
immune
impugn
oppugn
unhewn

(3)
picayune

UNG

bung
clung
dung
flung
hung
lung

rung
slung
sprung
strung
stung
sung
swung
tongue
wrung
young

(2)
among
oxtongue
unsprung
unstrung
unsung

UNK

funk
hunk
junk
monk
plunk
punk
shrunk
skunk
slunk
spunk
stunk
sunk
trunk

(2)
adunc
chipmunk
debunk
unshrunk

UNT

blunt
brunt
bunt
dunt
front
grunt
hunt
lunt
punt
runt
shunt
stunt

(2)
affront
confront

UP

cup
pup
sup
tup
up

(2)
kingcup
letup
markup
oilcup

(3)
follow-up
wickiup

UPT

cupped
supped

(2)
abrupt
bankrupt
corrupt
disrupt
erupt

(3)
incorrupt
interrupt

UR

blur
bur
burr
cur
err
fir
fur
her
knur
myrrh
per
purr
sir
slur
spur
stir
were
whir

(2)
astir
aver
bestir
concur
confer
defer
demur

deter
incur
infer
inter
larkspur
liqueur
longspur
masseur
monsieur
occur
recur
refer
transfer

(3)
cocklebur
connoisseur
disinter
raconteur
saboteur

URB

blurb
curb
herb
verb

(2)
adverb
disturb
perturb
superb

URCH

birch
church
curch
lurch
perch

search
smirch

(2)
besmirch
unchurch

URD

bird
curd
gird
heard
herd
third
word

(2)
absurd
begird
bellbird
cowbird
cowherd
lovebird

(3)
afterward
bowerbird
butcherbird
counterword
friarbird
ladybird
mockingbird
netherward
ovenbird
undergird

URE*

cure
lure

pure
sure

(2)
adjure
allure
assure
conjure
demure
endure
ensure
immure
impure
insure
inure
manure
mature
obscure
secure
unsure

(3)
epicure
manicure

URGE

dirge
merge
purge
scourge
serge
splurge
spurge
surge
urge
verge

(2)
converge

diverge
emerge
immerge
resurge
submerge
upsurge

(3)
demiurge
tramaturge
thaumaturge

URK

clerk
dirk
irk
jerk
kirk
lurk
murk
perk
quirk
shirk
smirk
work

(2)
berserk

URL

burl
churl
curl
earl
furl
girl
hurl
pearl
purl

skirl
swirl
twirl
whirl
whorl

(2)
cowgirl
impearl
uncurl
unfurl

URM

firm
germ
sperm
squirm
term
therm
worm

(2)
affirm
confirm
midterm
muckworm

(3)
disaffirm
isotherm

URN

burn
churn
earn
erne
fern
learn
spurn

stern
tern
turn
urn
yearn

(2)
adjourn
astern
attorn
concern
discern
epergne
interne
nocturne
return
sauterne
unlearn
upturn

(3)
overturn
taciturn

URSE

burse
curse
hearse
nurse
purse
terse
verse
worse

(2)
adverse
amerce
asperse
averse
coerce

converse
disburse
disperse
diverse
immerse
inverse
obverse
perverse
rehearse
reverse
sesterce
submerse
transverse
traverse

(3)
intersperse
reimburse
universe

URST

burst
durst
first
thirst
worst

(2)
athirst
emersed
cloudburst
inburst

URT

blurt
curt
dirt
flirt
girt

hurt
pert
quirt
shirt
skirt
spurt
squirt
wort

(2)
advert
alert
assert
avert
concert
convert
desert
dessert
dissert
divert
exert
expert
inert
insert
invert
obvert
outskirt
overt
pervert
revert
subvert
ungirt

(3)
antevert
controvert
disconcert
extravert
introvert
overskirt

preconcert
reconvert
undershirt
underskirt

URTH

berth
birth
dearth
earth
firth
girth
mirth
worth

(2)
inearth
rebirth
unearth

URVE

nerve
serve
swerve
verve

(2)
conserve
deserve
disserve
hors d'oeuvre
incurve
innerve
observe
outcurve
preserve
reserve
subserve
unnerve

US

bus
cuss
fuss
muss
plus
pus
thus
truss
us

(2)
discuss
nonplus
percuss

(3)
omnibus

USH

blush
brush
crush
flush
gush
hush
lush
mush
plush
rush
slush
thrush
tush

USK

brusque
busk
cusk

dusk
husk
musk
rusk
tusk

UST

bust
crust
dust
gust
just
lust
must
rust
thrust
trust

(2)
adjust
combust
disgust
distrust
encrust
entrust
mistrust
robust
unjust

UT

but
butt
cut
glut
gut
hut
jut
mutt

nut
putt
rut
scut
shut
slut
smut
strut

(2)
abut
besmut
crosscut
doughnut
englut
rebut
uncut

(3)
butternut
candlenut
coconut
scuttlebutt
undercut
uppercut

UTCH

clutch
crutch
dutch
hutch
much
scutch♦
such
touch

UTE*

butte
chute

cute
lute
mute

(2)
acute
astute
commute
compute
confute
depute
dilute
dispute
refute
repute
salute
transmute
tribute

(3)
attribute
constitute
destitute
disrepute
dissolute
execute
institute
malamute
parachute
persecute
prosecute
prostitute
substitute

UTH (see OOTH)

UV

dove
glove

love
of
shove

(2)
above
thereof
truelove

(3)
ladylove
turtledove
light-o'-love

UX

crux
flux
lux
tux

(2)
afflux
conflux
deluxe

UZ

buzz
does
fuzz
was

(2)
abuzz

ŪZ

cues
dues
fuse
hews

hues
mews
muse
news
pews
stews
thews
use
views

(2)
abuse
accuse
amuse
bemuse
confuse
contuse
diffuse
disuse
effuse
excuse
infuse
previews
refuse
suffuse
transfuse

UBBER

(2)
blubber
grubber
lubber
rubber
slubber

(3)
landlubber

UBBLE

(2)
bubble
hubble
nubble
rubble
stubble
trouble

*A laugh is worth
a hundred groans in any
market.* —Lamb

"LET NO MAN PUT ASUNDER"
*Because —
What man hath joined
is sure to be a blunder.*

***

THE CROSS I'D BEAR
*At church, my voice soared on the air,
As we sang, "Sweet Bye and Bye"
But as a child I always wondered why
We sang about "The Cross-Eyed Bear."*

***

BUT DON'T TELL A SOUL
*One sure way to keep gossip
alive is to give it mouth
to mouth resuscitation.*
—nm

UCKLE

(2)
buckle
huckle
knuckle
muckle
suckle
truckle

(3)
parbuckle
turnbuckle
unbuckle

(4)
honeysuckle

UCTION

(2)
suction

(3)
abduction
conduction
construction
deduction
destruction
induction
instruction
obstruction
production
reduction
substruction

(4)
introduction
reproduction

UCTOR

(3)
abductor
conductor
destructor
instructor
reductor

UDDER

(2)
budder
mudder
rudder
scudder
shudder
udder

UDDLE

(2)
cuddle
huddle
muddle
puddle

(3)
befuddle

UDDY

(2)
buddy
muddy
ruddy
study

(4
fuddy-duddy

UFFER

(2)
bluffer
buffer
duffer
puffer
rougher
suffer
tougher

UFFLE

(2)
duffel
muffle
ruffle
shuffle
truffle

UGGLE

(2)
juggle
smuggle
snuggle
struggle

ULSION

(3)
avulsion
compulsion
convulsion
devulsion
emulsion
expulsion
impulsion
repulsion
revulsion

UMBER

(2)
cumber
clumber
lumbar
lumber
number
slumber
umber

(3)
cucumber
encumber
outnumber

(4)
disencumber

UMBLE

(2)
bumble
crumble
fumble
grumble
humble
jumble
mumble
rumble
stumble
tumble

UMEN

(2)
human
numen
lumen

(3)
accumen
albumin
decuman
hegumen
ichneumon
illumine
subhuman

(4)
catechumen
energumen

superhuman

UMMER

(2)
comer
cummer
dumber
drummer
hummer
mummer
plumber
rummer
slummer
strummer
summer

UMMY

(2)
chummy
crummy
dummy
mummy
rummy
scummy
yummy

UMPER

(2)
bumper
dumper
jumper
lumper
plumper
thumper

UMPTION

(2)
gumption

(3)
consumption
presumption
resumption
subsumption

UNCTION

(2)
function
junction
unction

(3)
adjunction
compunction
conjunction
dysfunction
inunction
malfunction

UNDER

(2)
blunder
plunder
sunder
thunder
under
wonder

(3)
asunder
thereunder

UNKER

(2)
bunker
junker
plunker

(3)
debunker
spelunker

UNNER

(2)
gunner
punner
runner
shunner
stunner
sunner

(3)
forerunner

UNNY

(2)
bunny
funny
honey
money
runny
sunny

UPPER

(2)
cupper
crupper
scupper
supper
upper

URITY

(3)
curity
purity
surety

(4)
futurity
impurity
maturity
obscurity
security

URKY

(2)
jerky
murky
perky
turkey

URNAL

(2)
colonel
journal
kernel
sternal
vernal

(3)
eternal
infernal
maternal
nocturnal
paternal

URRY

(2)
curry
furry
hurry
scurry
surrey
worry

URSION

(2)
version

(3)
aspersion
emersion
excursion
immersion
incursion
inversion
obversion
perversion
subversion

USHER

(2)
crusher
flusher
gusher
musher
rusher
usher

(3)
fourflusher

USION

(2)
fusion

(3)
confusion

contusion
delusion
diffusion
effusion
exclusion
illusion
inclusion
infusion
intrusion
obtrusion
occlusion
perfusion
preclusion
prelusion
profusion
protrusion
reclusion
suffusion
transfusion

USTER

(2)
bluster
buster
cluster
duster
fluster
luster
muster

(4)
filibuster

USTLE

(2)
bustle
hustle
muscle

mussel
rustle
tussle

(3)
corpuscle

USTY

(2)
busty
crusty
dusty
gusty
lusty
musty
rusty
trusty

UTER

(2)
cuter
neuter
pewter

(3)
commuter
computer

(4)
persecutor
prolocutor
prosecutor
prostitutor

UTHER

(2)
brother
mother

other
smother

(3)
godmother
grandmother
housemother

UTION

(3)
ablution
pollution
solution

(4)
absolution
allocution
constitution
devolution
diminution
dissolution
elocution
obvolution
persecution
prosecution
prostitution
resolution
restitution
retribution
revolution

UTTER

(2)
butter
clutter
cutter
flutter
gutter
mutter

putter
scutter
shutter
sputter
stutter
utter

UTTLE

(2)
cuttle
scuttle
shuttle
subtle

(3)
abuttal
rebuttal

UVER

(2)
cover
glover
hover
lover

(3)
discover
recover
uncover
windhover

(4)
undercover

OF EARTHLY CYCLES

Aging lilac
bush stands
proudly,
waiting for
spring
and new
finery.

***

April fooled
early spring
buds with
snow; winter
gave its
grand
finale.

***

White petunia—
the ladybug's
parasol;
shelter from
cold rain.

***

Leaves
flutter excitedly;
they are dressed
for October's grand
parade.

—nm

Part II

HELPS FOR THE POET

Glossary of Poetic Terms

ablaut change of vowels in verbal forms, showing tense, as sink, sank, sunk. Also called gradation.

acute accent in poetry, the primary stress on a syllable.

alliteration in modern poetry, the repetition of initial sound, usually a consonant.

amphibrach a long syllable between two short ones, as in *amusement*.

amphimacer a short syllable between two long ones, as in *diadem*.

anacoluthon a change from one grammatical construction to another in the same sentence.

Anacreontic a verse in ABAB rhyme and rhythm; a form used by the Greek poet, Anacreon.

anacrusis variation in syllable count; unaccented syllable(s) added at the beginning of a line that ordinarily starts with an accented syllable.

anadiplosis repetition of a key word, especially the last one, at the beginning of a clause or sentence, as "She wrote poetry; poetry was her life."

anapest two short syllables, followed by a long one; a line of verse using this foot.

anaphera repeating a word or phrase at the beginning of successive clauses or sentences.

antistrophe in a Pindaric ode, that part which follows the strophe.

antonym a word whose meaning is opposite to that of another, as cold is the antonym of hot.

aphorism a short sentence expressing a precept or truth.

apocope dropping the last syllable or letter of a word, as lan' for land.

aposiopesis a sudden stop or breaking off in the middle of a sentence, as "The plane crash was horrible—oh, I can't talk about it."

apostrophe words addressed to a person or thing, whether absent or present.

arsis the accented part of a foot of verse; used in this manner because of a misinterpretation of the original Greek word.

assonance a partial rhyme, in which stressed vowels have the same sound, but the consonants are different, as *coarse, source*.

Bragi in Norse mythology, the son of Oden and Frigga; god of poetry.

caesura a break in a line; in scansion it is indicated by two short vertical lines.

Calliope in Greek mythology, the Muse of epic poetry.

canzone a lyric poem of Italian origin; resembles a madrigal.

conzonet a short, lively song.

caret a mark used to show that something is to be added.

catalexis in trochaic and dactyllic verse, a light syllable is lacking at the end of the line.

cedilla a small, hooklike mark, attached to the letter *c* to show that it is to be pronounced like a voiceless *s*, as in *soupçon*.

chain lanterne a form originated by Monica Boyce. It is a double lanterne, with the second stanza starting with the last word of the first stanza. More stanzas may be added, keeping to the above rules. It may have a title, if desired, See lanterne.

choriamb a foot of four syllables; the first and last are stressed, the middle two, unstressed.

cinquain a poem of five lines of two, four, six, eight and two syllables. It was originated by Adeliade Crapsey (1878-1914) and is called an American version of the tanka.

clerihew a humorous verse originated by Edward Clerihew Bentley. Its rhyme scheme is AABB. The first line uses a famous historical figure. The action must be fictitious. This form has no title.

colophon an inscription giving facts about the production of a book; also a publisher's trademark.

consonance harmony; combination of pleasant sounds.

couplet two lines of poetry having the same rhyme.

cretic see amphimacer.

dactyl a foot of three syllables, the first accented, the others unaccented.

dagger in printing, this is a reference mark; the double dagger is also used.

desinence a termination; suffix.

dieresis the mark (″) placed over the second vowel of a diphthong, showing that it is to be pronounced as two syllables.

digraph two letters that represent one sound, as *ph* in *telephone*.

dissonance lacking harmony; discord.

dissyllable a word of two syllables.

distich a unit of two lines of verse; couplet.

dithyramb an emotional song or writing.

doggerel a trivial verse, usually comical in nature; a jingle.

eclogue a short pastoral poem.

elision the omission or slurring of a vowel or syllable; used in poetry when a word ends in a vowel before another word beginning with a vowel or silent *h*.

enclitic a word that loses its natural stress when combined with another word, as *doorman*.

enjambment running on of one sentence to another line without pause at the end of a line.

epic a long narrative poem about heroic or historic persons.

epigram a short poem, witty or satirical.

epitaph a short verse written as a tribute to a dead person.

epithalamium a poem in honor of a bride or groom—or both.

epode a lyric poem. This form was used by Horace, the Roman poet.

eponym a real or mythical person whose name is given to a nation or institution. Also a person whose name is associated with a movement or period, as *Victorian* period, after Queen Victoria.

epopoeia epopee; the making of epic poetry.

Euterpe in Greek mythology, the Muse of music and lyric poetry.

Erato in Greek mythology, the Muse of lyric and love poetry.

feminine ending an unstressed syllable at the end of a line.

gest/geste a story of adventure, written in verse.

grave accent used to indicate a secondary stress; also for full pronunciation of a syllable normally slurred in speech, as in *belovèd*.

hemistich a half-line of verse, before or after the caesura.

hexameter a line of six metrical feet.

hexastich poem or stanza of six lines.

Hippocrene a fountain on Mount Helicon, whose waters are supposed to inspire poets.

Homer a Greek epic poet who lived in the eighth century B.C.

Horace a Roman poet (65-8 B.C.) known for his odes.

hymeneal a wedding song or poem.

hypercatalectic an additional unaccented syllable or two, following the natural close of the verse.

iamb a foot of two syllables, the first unaccented, the second accented, as in *demure*.

imagination the act of creating images of what has never been experienced; often considered the greatest creative power.

inversion often called "forced rhyme" because it reverses the normal order of words. It was once used to complete a rhyme scheme, but is not considered good form in modern poetry. Example: "As bread was never to the hungry given."

ionic, greater This foot has four syllables, the first two are long and the second two are short; used mostly in Greek and Latin poetry.

ionic, lesser Here the stress is reversed, first syllables being short, the others long.

iowetta a poem of three stanzas. Each stanza is made of two couplets in iambic tetrameter and one line in iambic pentameter. The three pentameter lines all have the same rhyme. The subject is generally irony, fantasy, or adventure. Originated by Nel Modglin.

lampoon a drinking song, ridiculing someone.

lanterne This short poem, about nature, was originated by Lloyd Frank Merrill. The syllable count is 1, 2, 3, 4, 1.

lavelle a poem made of couplets and tercets, in the following order: couplet, tercet, tercet, tercet, couplet, couplet. The first and last couplets have identical rhymes. This poem is written in iambic tetrameter lines; it was originated by Nel Modglin.

lay a short narrative poem that can be sung.

lene a smooth consonant.

limerick a nonsensical or light verse having three long and two short lines. The rhyme is AABBA. This form was made popular by Edward Lear.

litotes a figure in which something is expressed by negation, as "his visit is no rare occurrence," meaning his visits are frequent.

logaoedic The meter is a combination of dactyls and trochees, or anapests and iambics.

logogram a symbol used to represent a word, as *c* for cents.

logomachy an argument about words; the game of anagrams.

lyric Sonnets, hymns, elegies, and odes are some of the forms classified as lyric poetry. They are generally about personal emotions, rather than external events.

macron from the Greek work *makros* ("long"); a mark over a vowel to indicate that it is to be pronounced in that manner.

macaronic a mixture of language in which coined words from two or more languages are used; burlesque verse.

madrigal a short poem that can be set to music; generally, it has a love theme.

mānardina a poem of twelve iambic lines, having 4, 8, 8, 8, 8, 4/4, 8, 8, 8, 8, 4 syllables. First and last lines must rhyme. The third, fourth, ninth and tenth lines must also rhyme, but not with the first and last lines. This form was originated by Nel Modglin.

melic In Greek poetry, this form is to be sung.

metaphrase a literal translation.

metaphrast one who changes a writing, as prose to poetry.

metaphor a figure of speech in which one thing is spoken of as if it were the other.

metonym one word substituted for another, as "The White House reported," meaning the president reported.

metrist a poet who writes in meter.

mixed metaphor using two or more metaphors in an inconsistent manner, as "He was mad as a hornet, but his anger was nipped in the bud."

molossus a classical foot.

monody a poem lamenting death.

monologue a poem in which one character does all the speaking.

monophthong a single vowel sound.

monosyllable a word of one syllable.

morpheme a word that cannot be divided into smaller parts and still convey meaning.

neologism new words or new meanings for established words.

obelus a mark used to indicate questionable passages; a reference mark. See dagger.

octameter a line that contains eight metrical feet.

ode originally, a poem to be sung, now a lyric, rhymed or unrhymed, addressed to someone. Used by the poet Pindar.

oenomel a strong, sweet speech.

onomatopoeia formation of a word that imitates sound, as *buzz*.

orthoepy the branch of grammar dealing with pronunciation.

orthographer an expert speller.

oxymoron a figure of speech in which opposite terms are used, as "roaring silence."

oxytone a word with the acute accent on the last syllable.

paean a song of triumph and joy.

paeon a foot of three short syllables and one long syllable, in any order.

palindrome a word or sentence that reads the same backward or forward.

palinode an ode or song that retracts something that has been previously written.

paragoge adding a letter or syllable at the end of a word.

paraphrase rewording of something said or written before.

pararhyme one of many terms for near rhyme. Other names are "oblique," "off rhyme" or "slant rhyme."

Parnassus a mountain in Greece sacred to Apollo and the Muses; therefore the word is used to mean the center of poetic activity.

paronym one word of a pair derived from the same root.

paronymous refers to words different in spelling and meaning, but pronounced alike, as *see, sea.*

paroxytone a word having the accent on the next to last syllable.

pasquinade a lampoon, usually posted in public.

pathetic fallacy the poetic device of giving inanimate objects human qualities, as "the angry wind."

patois a blend of dialect with standard forms of language.

Pegasus according to Greek mythology, a winged horse that issued from the dead body of Medusa. Poetic inspiration.

perfect rhyme two syllables or words that are spelled or pronounced alike, but have different meanings, as *yew, you.* Also called "rich rhyme."

persiflage a frivolous style of speaking or writing; banter, flippancy.

personification an object, idea, or quality represented as a person. Also used when one intends to express a perfect example: "She is the personification of beauty."

Pindar a Greek poet (522?-443 B.C.) who is known for his odes; characteristic of Pindar's style.

postpositive placed after another word, or added to it; suffixed.

proclitic a word that has no accent of its own, but is pronounced with the word that follows.

proem a preface or introduction, generally brief.

prosody the poet's style of versification, as meter, stanza, rhyme; choice of words.

prosopopoeia a figure of speech in which a dead or imaginary person is supposed to be speaking; personification.

pure poetry writing that does not try to instruct, convert, or improve the reader.

pyrrhic two short or unstressed syllables.

redundant repetitive; more than enough needed to make the meaning clear.

rhematic of or derived from a verb.

rhetoric the art of using words in speaking or writing; artificial eloquence.

rhetorician teacher of rhetoric; one who writes or speaks in showy language.

rondeau a poem of thirteen lines, in three stanzas, composed in two rhymes. The first and last stanzas have five lines, the second three. It has an unrhymed refrain, after second and third stanzas, made from the opening words of the first line. This is a French form and generally written in tetrameter. The rhyme scheme is AABBA/AABR/ABBAR.

Sapphic a stanza of three five-stress lines, followed by a short line.

Sappho a female poet of ancient Greece, famous for her love lyrics.

scansion analyzing poetry, counting accent or stress and metrical feet; determining the rhythm.

scazon a six-footed iambic line, with the final foot reversed.

schwa the unstressed central vowel of most unstressed syllables, as the *e* in *urgent*.

semantics a part of linguistics concerned with structure and development of speech forms.

semasiology signification of a word; semantics.

semivowel a vowel used as a consonant, as *y* and *w*.

simile a figure of speech in which one thing is likened to another, as "Her heart is like a stone."

solecism substandard use of words, as "He has went."

sonnet Classed as a lyric, it is a poem of fourteen iambic lines. The Petrarchan, English and Spenserian are the established forms. Two modern forms are the Illini and Mason.

sonnet, Illini This form varies in syllable count, having 8, 10, 10, 8/8, 10, 10, 8/8, 10, 10, 8/10, 10 per line. The rhyme scheme is ABCA/BCDC/CDEC/EE. Nel Modglin invented this sonnet.

sonnet, Mason fourteen iambic lines. Rhyme scheme: ABCA/BCCB/DBAD/DA. Madeline Mason invented this form.

sonnette seven iambic lines. Rhyme scheme is ABAB/CDC. Sherman Ripley invented this form.

spondee a metrical foot of two accented syllables.

strophe a stanza. In a Pindaric ode, the stanza that is answered by the antistrophe.

syllabary a set of written characters that represent spoken syllables.

synecdoche a figure of speech in which a part is used for the whole—or the whole used as a part; e.g., "a pair of ragged claws" (from "The Love Song of J. Alfred Prufrock"—T.S. Eliot)

syneresis the contracting of two vowels or syllables into one syllable.

synonym one of a pair of words having the same (or nearly the same) meaning in one or more senses; opposite of antonym.

syntax the branch of grammar dealing with the arrangement of words; sentence structure.

tanka a Japanese form, older than the haiku. It is a poem of five lines; syllable count is 5, 7, 5, 7, 7. It is used for love and nature themes, also personal philosophy.

tautology repetition of the same idea in different words; redundancy.

tercet three lines of poetry, all having the same rhyme.

tetrabrach a foot, or a word, having four short syllables.

tetrameter a line having four feet or measures.

tetrastich a stanza or poem having four lines.

tetrasyllable a word having four syllables.

Thalia one of the three Graces; in Greek mythology, the Muse of comedy and pastoral poetry.

thesis now considered to be the unaccented syllable in a foot. This is due to a misunderstanding of the Greek word.

threnody a funeral song.

tilde In Spanish, this mark is used over an *ñ* to indicate that it is to be pronounced *ny,* as in *ñizca.*

tmesis the separation of compound words by inserting another word or words.

tribrach a metrical foot of three syllables.

triolet a poem made of two quatrains and using only two rhymes. The first line is repeated as the fourth and seventh lines. The second line is repeated for the eighth, or final line.

trigraph three letters representing one sound, as *eau* in *rondeau.*

trimeter a line having three metrical feet.

triphthong the use of three vowels in one syllable.

trochee a metrical foot containing one long syllable, followed by a short one. "Many soldiers choose to perish," is a trochaic line.

typology the study of types or symbols.

verse a line of poetry; erroneously used to mean a stanza. Verse also means poetry in general.

verse de societé witty, sophisticated verse.

versicle generally a little verse sung by a minister and followed by a response from the congregation.

vers libre Free verse does not use rhyme, but it must be rhythmic. Considered by many poets to be the most difficult poetry to write successfully.

villanelle a French form of nineteen lines in two rhymes. It has six stanzas. The first and third lines of the first tercet are used alternately as the end lines of the other tercets. The last stanza is a quatrain, concluding with the first and third lines, with the first line of the poem becoming the third line of the quatrain and the last line of the first stanza becoming the last line of the poem.

virelay a French form, having two rhymes; its two opening lines are repeated at intervals. It is also a jingle used at the end of a song.

virgule a diagonal mark between words as *and/or,* which indicates that either word can be used.

vision speaking of that which is distant or past or future, as if it were before one at the moment, as "I see Christians being thrown to the lions."

words sounds that express thought. They have tones, like notes in music.

zodiacal verse a modern form originated by Vivian Meyer. The last letters of the lines must spell your astrological sign. Incorporate your moon sign at birth, if you know it; otherwise use another. Do not rhyme. Any subject may be used.

Six Modern Poetry Forms

by Monica Boyce, Vivian Meyer, and Nel Modglin

A CHAIN LATERNE*

(Originated by Monica Boyce)

The
soft voice
of silence
slithers 'round
the bereaved with
guile.
Guile
subtle
and deadly
has serpentine
ways.

—nm

---

* Rules for the chain-laterne are on page 116. Monica Boyce is the editor of *Parnassus* magazine.

ILLINI SONNET*

(Originated by Nel Modglin)

MARCH AND EARLY VIOLETS

A high-rise occupies the ground
Where last March I picked early violets.
Today faint redolence perfumes the air
As zephyrs rouse past springtimes drowned
In time. (Progressing, man forgets,
But hints of prior vernal days are there.)
This is such a day of ghosts returning;
They stir the pool where vague regrets
Keep company with dark despair.
Phantoms of dead years wake poignant yearning.
As honeybees glean nectar, spectral wings
Cast shadows, making one aware
That violets are fundamental things;
Bricks crumble, but bees fly in ceaseless
                        springs.

—Thelma Scott Kiser

---

* Rules for the Illini sonnet are on page 122.

THE IOWETTA
(Originated by Nel Modglin)

IN AND OUT WITH ME

Oh, I know the Preşence is there,
Though it is flesh-and-boned with air.
I say its teachings are musty,
But find them to be gold-dusty.
Denying this truth only shows my hand.

My Mentor has a subtle voice
And lets me make the final choice.
Therefore, when I go astraying,
I know IT is there, waylaying,
Ready with swift, unsubtle reprimand.

My faithful Other never sleeps.
It listens in and always keeps
A record of night's long dreaming,
Lest the day be filled to teeming
With ghosts that frighten with dark's
                              contraband.

—nm

THE LAVELLE*

(Originated by Nel Modglin)

THIS INWARD LOOK

The joys of life I do not see
Are things so very close to me . . .

A tall pine tree, a grassy slope,
A little child with eyes of hope,
Or bunny rabbit's graceful lope.

The sunshine and the falling rain;
The harvest of sweet golden grain
That comes and goes and comes again.

Unconsciously, they are passed by
Without a thought or rueful sigh:
Careless of me? I wonder why.

The wet dews come and then arise
To meet the clouds to my surprise . . .

This inward look of self should be
The key to set my conscience free.

—Isabel H. Lancaster

* Rules for the lavelle are on page 118.

THE MĀNARDINA*

(Originated by Nel Modglin)

GRETCHEN

She kicks the night,
toe poking below subterrains,
with hands stroking, in liquid tone,
the lactic world, the moon—cold stone—
taut, ticking nine-month days away . . .
Arms clutch at space
that she not fall,
lost, from limbs of her beginnings.
Genesis gathers in the bone,
becomes ONENESS. Exodus, lone,
heads through the hurting gate, clay-blue,
blinking at light.

—Marjorie Culver

* Rules for the mānardina are on page 119.

ZODIACAL VERSE*

(Originated by Vivian Meyer)

FURY OF LOVE AND HATE

Her words were like the cooing of doves,
But her touch burned like carbolic
Acid. Why, he implored, did they go
on hurting each other?
We are caught in a kind of trap,
She replied. Being a Gemini
Of love and hate, we make an emotional
                                    inferno.

                                —nm

---

*Rules for zodiacal verse are on page 124. Vivian Meyers is president of the New Jersey Poetry Society.

What Is Meter?

The word stems from the Greek word *metron,* meaning measure. Therefore, meter in verse is a pattern of syllables, arranged by stress.

Monometer: one foot
Dimeter: two feet
Trimeter: three feet
Tetrameter: four feet

Pentameter: five feet
Hexameter: six feet
Heptameter: seven feet
Octameter: eight feet

POETIC FEET*

Amphibrach	-/-
Amphimacer	/-/
Anapest	--/
Choriamb**	/--/
Dactyl	/--
Iamb	-/
Ionic (greater)	//--
(lesser)	--//
Paeon***	---/
Pyrrhic	--
Spondee	//
Tetrabrach	----
Tribrach	---
Trochee	/-

* This sign (-) represents a short foot. This sign (/) represents a long foot.

** Choriambs are used in Greek and Latin verse.

*** A paeon may also be in reverse order.

Giving Your Poem a Title

Give your poem a name. Designating your work as a poem, sonnet, or rondeau indicates that the readers would not know a sonnet or rondeau unless you told them what they were reading!

To tag your poem with the word *Untitled* is to say, in effect, that you don't know what you are writing about and the reader must decide for himself. (If the reader bothers at all, for one of the main purposes of a title is to catch the reader's attention.)

However, the title should not be too cute or misleading; often it is the key to the poem's meaning.

Try not to use trite, overdone titles; be as original as possible, for this is, after all, the introduction to what you have written.

Many authorities suggest that one-word titles, such as "Winter," "Grief" and "Sunset," should not be used. Keeping in mind that the title is the first thing an editor sees, you will try to select one that will hold his attention long enough for the first line to be read.

The title chosen, then, is the poem's advertising. Make it as truthful, but as attractive, as possible.

Oriental Poetry Forms

The oldest of oriental poetry forms is the Chinese prose form used in their folk songs. Then came the very intricate and sophisticated quatrains and the sixteen-syllable song-poems of Tzu, which are believed to have inspired the haiku.

Japanese poetry also started with folks songs and the "long" poems, Choka or Naga Uta, seldom longer than forty lines. But whatever form, the poems are always written in an alternative five-syllable or seven-syllable form, and are always unrhymed. Their grammar is terse; the language used, unsophisticated. The oldest of the short forms, the Sedoka (5-7-7, 5-7-7 syllables) was used for the observation and interpretation of nature and was popular during the first part of the eighth century. Example:

LOST LOVE

Aloes wood perfume
clings to the silken covers
in the chamber of my love—
her flesh gives back its fragrance.

In vain, in vain now
the golden oriole sings—
she comes no more to linger
under the low chestnut tree.

Another form is the Dodoitsu (also called Minyo) of 7-7-7-5 syllables; it is a throwback to the old folk songs, and became popular during the twelfth century. It is the form used by the people and workers. Example:

RENDEZVOUS

White pidgeons in ancient pines
clutter less than this shy heart
waiting at the water clock
for your late coming.

—Jean's Journal

The tanka (5-7-5-7-7 syllables) is an older form than the haiku and still is the official form for poetry competitions in Japan. It is used for love themes, personal musings or philosophy, as well as nature obervations. Example:

FAITHFUL

As mallard ducks sleep
white wing overlapping wing—
against early frost
curve your arms around me, love,
as the long rains turn to snow.

—Modern Images

Other forms are haiku and senryu. The haiku is thought to have emerged in its present form sometime during the thirteenth century. It is a nature observation, portraying a moment of awareness.

The senryu has the same syllable count (5-7-5) but is satirical or whimsical, dealing with human faults and foibles.

There is the klong form, used in Thailand and the Philippines, and the sijo form of Korea, both so intricate that much study is required to master them.

—Magny Landstad Jensen

TEACHER, THIS DARKNESS*

You doubted me,
I think, but patiently explained:
"Words cannot describe green on green,"
you said. "Penetrating that screen
is difficult, but then comes your
clarity. Light
becomes almost
tangible; it intoxicates.
Once, having truly heard and seen,
all clouds disperse that come between."
Teacher, it's true. I did not hear,
nor do I see.

                                                                                        nm

---

*Rules for the mānardina are on page 119.

Bring Me My Bow of Burning Gold——

Yes, poets, in William Blake's memorable words, bring your bows, but aim carefully. Too, look to the gold and to the burning, that they be real.

For we're heirs to poetry, to a universe of spinning spheres in which all energy and force flow in rising and falling measure. That man responds rhythmically to the organic patterns that control him is as inevitable as dark and light, winter and summer, life and death, as irresistible as his heartbeat, his breathing in and out again.

What is a poem? In what ways does it differ from prose?

1. Of all the language arts, it is the most intense, most compressed.
2. It is a process, a creation, of an inner power, a heightened awareness, fused with disciplined technique. It is art and craft in which mind, emotion, and instinct are all present.
3. The poet probes experience for *essence,* freeing himself from all precepts of thought and expression. It is a process of *becoming.*
4. The poem implies beyond words, reaching for deeper meaning.
5. Beyond interpretation, the poem needs no explanation.
6. It sets up echoes in the ear, the mind, the heart, sometimes the subconscious.
7. The poem uses sound, silences, stresses, to set the tone, the meaning, the mood.
8. The poet uses poetic devices with knowledge and skill—metaphor, symbol, rhyme, rhythm, form, image.
9. Rhythmically patterned language, the natural rhythms of speech, vital, fresh, original, uniquely one's own, are the ingredients of poetry.
10. As the poet grows to an ever-deepening awareness, his words

will reach toward universality, a quality present in all great poetry. Meaning depends on the totality perceived in all things.

To judge your poem, ask yourself:
1. Does it move? Or is it static, dead? Dull?
2. Is it essentially you? Alive? Individual?
3. Is it burdened with clichés, wearied usages?
4. Does it wallow in sentimentality? Is it guilty of affectation, floweriness, pretentiousness?
5. Is it the same old theme, said in the same old way? Or have you contributed new insights, enriched it with an awakened awareness?
6. Have you used sing-song rhymes, stereotyped rhythms? Or have you found the measure and sound exactly right for your words, your meaning?
7. Have you used inversions, forced rhyme?
8. Is the poem weakened or destroyed with overstatement, pallid emotionalism, false statement? Editorializing?
9. Have you watched for over-use of alliteration, mixed metaphor, or other ineptitudes in handling of poetic devices?
10. Does the essence of the experience emerge, free of all trimmings, that the experience (which may be old as time) be brought forth, a creation vital with new meaning?

There are three levels of poetry, sometimes a fourth.
1. *The Literal Level.* This is the sensual level of sight, hearing, taste, feel, smell. Much contemporary poetry is written at this level, in which experience projects through sensual description. Meanings often exist beneath this level.
2. *The Metaphoric Level.* Poetry sometimes manages a new vision of the world by means of comparison or analogy. Simile, metaphor, symbol, image are used, often comparing things surprisingly dissimilar, but alike in one way. Indirections or paradox, metaphor, symbol, are often used to achieve a more complex truth.
3. *The Statement Level.* This is a difficult level for poets, for it must be backed up with proof: literal and metaphoric levels. Unless this is done, the poem proves nothing to the reader. There is danger of triteness at all levels, in the *literal,* hazards of flatness, dullness, poor selection of detail. At the *metaphoric level,* we find danger of irrelevance, since the device used should contribute to the tone

or feeling of the poem. *Statement level* is most hazardous because it is imperative it be proved.

4. *The Transcendental Level.* This may be a fourth level for a successful poem, in which implications go beyond the literal level of the poem. This quality may rarely be striven for; its connotations occasionally enrich the exceptional poem.

In conclusion, poets, remember to guard your *difference*. It is the stuff of poetry. Love the language, selecting every word with infinite care. Accept no stereotypes; reach for the unknown, a new knowing. Listen to the sound of yourself—hear your words, sound out your rhythms. What does the title do for the poem? Often it is the clue that solves the mystery. What is the spirit of the poem? Is the tone consistent and right for this particular poem? Is your poem evocative, reaching the reader? Have you indulged in verbosity, in verbal histrionics? Is your poem honest, original, perceptive? Does it say beyond its words, in a oneness of mood, the true, the elusive, the unsayable?

—Marjorie Culver
Poet, Editor, Teacher

A BUD IN LOVE'S BOUQUET
An Illini Sonnet

"My name is Mebba," said the child
To everyone who passed along the street.
I stopped, one time, and tried to talk
                          with her
And was, somehow, strangely beguiled.
The lesson learned is bittersweet;
I feel, again, the sting of guilt bestir.
"Mentally retarded," I said that day,
"But so exquisitely petite."
Though many never will concur,
I think she is a bud in Love's bouquet,
For who can judge Lou Melba's inner sight
Or know the truth it will confer?
Perhaps it is a longer, darker night
Out here, where I stand, at her fence of
                          light.

—nm

INDEX TO THE RHYMER

Index

A	3, 4	ANE	13, 14	AUSE	22
AB	4	ANG	14	AVE	22
ACE	4, 5	ANGE	15	AWE	22
ACK	5	ANK	15	AWK	22, 23
ACT	5	ANT	15	AWN	23
AD	6	AP	15, 16	AZE	23
ADE	6, 7	APE	16	AZH	23
AFE	7	APSE	16	ABBER	24
AFF	7	APT	16	ABBLE	24
AFT	7	AR	16	ABBY	24
AG	7, 8	ARCH	16	ABLE	24
AGE	8	ARD	16, 17	ABOR	24
AID	6, 7	ARE	8, 9	ACEOUS	24
AIL	9, 10	ARGE	17	ACITY	24
AIM	11	ARK	17	ACKER	24
AIN	13, 14	ARM	17	ACKLE	24, 25
AINT	8	ARP	17	ACTION	25
AIR	8, 9	ART	17, 18	ACTOR	25
AIT	20, 21	ASH	18	ADDER	25
AKE	9	ASK	18	ADDLE	25
AL	9	ASP	18	AGGLE	25
ALE	9, 10	ASS	18	AGGY	25
ALL	10	AST	18, 19	AILER	25
ALM	10, 11	ASTE	19	AINER	25, 26
ALT	11	AT	19	AKER	26
AM	11	ATCH	19, 20	ALITY	26
AME	11	ATE	20, 21	ALLIC	26
AMP	11, 12	ATH	21	ALLION	26
AN	12	AUD	21	ALLOW	26
ANCE	12, 13	AUGHT	88	AMBLE	26
ANCH	13	AUNCH	22	AMMER	26, 27
AND	13	AUNT	22	AMPER	27

AMPLE	27	EAM	38	ERTH	105
ANCER	27	EAN	38	ERVE	105
ANDER	27	EAP	39	ESH	44
ANDLE	27	EAR	39	ESS	44
ANDY	27	EASE	46	EST	44, 45
ANGER	27	EAST	34	ET	45
ANGLE	27, 28	EAT	40	ETCH	45, 46
ANGLER	28	EATH	34	ETE	40
ANIC	28	EATHE	35	EVE	46
ANISH	28	ECE	35	EX	46
ANJER	28	ECK	35	EZ	46
ANKER	28	ECT	35, 36	EACHER	47
ANNER	28	ED	36	EADER	48
ANTER	28	EDE	36, 37	EAGLE	47
ANTIC	28	EDGE	36	EAKER	48
APER	28, 29	EED	36, 37	EALER	48
APPER	29	EEF	37	EAMER	48
APPY	29	EEK	37	EANER	48
ARITY	29	EEL	37, 38	EAPER	48
ARKER	29	EEM	38	EATER	48
ARMER	29	EEN	38, 39	EATHER	47
ARROW	29	EEP	39	EAVEN	47
ARRY	29	EER	39	EAVER	49
ARTER	29	EET	40	ECTION	47
ARY	29, 30	EETH	34	ECTIVE	48
ASHER	30	EFT	40	EDDLE	48
ASION	30	EIGHT	20, 21	EEDER	48
ASSION	30, 31	ELD	40	EEKER	48
ASTER	31	ELL	40, 41	EELER	48
ATHER	31	ELT	41	EEMER	48
ATIC	31	ELVES	41	EENER	48
ATION	31, 32	EM	41	EEPER	48
ATOR	32	EN	41, 42	EETER	48
ATTER	32	ENCE	42	EEVER	49
ATTLE	32	ENCH	42	ELLER	49
AVEL	32	END	42, 43	ELLOW	49
AVER	32, 33	ENT	43	ELTER	49
AVITY	33	EPT	43, 44	ENDER	49
AZER	33	ER	102	ENTAL	49
AZY	33	ERD	102	ENTER	50
		ERE	39	ENTION	50
		ERGE	103	ENTURE	50
E	33, 34	ERM	103	EPTION	50
EACH	34	ERN	103, 104	ERIC	50
EAD	36, 37	ERSE	104	ERIOR	50
EAK	37	ERST	104	ERITY	50
EAL	37, 38	ERT	104, 105	ERRY	50, 51

ESSION	51	IRE	60, 61	INGER	69
ESSOR	51	IRK	103	INGLE	69
ESTER	51	IRL	103	INION	69
ETIC	51	IRM	103	INIT	69
ESTLE	51	IRST	104	INITY	69
ETION	51	IRT	104, 105	INJER	69
ETTER	51, 52	IRTH	105	INKER	69
ETTLE	52	ISH	61	INKLE	69, 70
EVEL	52	ISK	61	INNER	70
EVER	52	ISS	61	IPPER	70
		IST	61, 62	IPPLE	70
		IT	62	IPTION	70
I	52, 53	ITCH	62, 63	ISER	70
IBE	53	ITE	63	ISION	70
ICE	53	ITH	63, 64	ISSION	70, 71
ICH	62, 63	IVE	64	ISSLE	71
ICK	54	IX	64	ISTER	71
ICT	54	IZE	64, 65	ISTIC	71
ID	54	IBBLE	65	ITER	71
IDE	54, 55	IBLE	65	ITHER	71
IEVE	40	ICIOUS	65	ITIC	71
IFE	55	ICIT	65	ITTEN	72
IFF	55	ICITY	65	ITTER	72
IFT	55	ICKER	65, 66	ITTLE	72
IG	55, 56	ICKLE	66	ITTY	72
IGHT	63	ICTION	66	IVER	72
IKE	56	IDDEN	66	IZZARD	72
ILD	56	IDDLE	66	IZZLE	72
ILE	56	IDER	66		
ILL	56, 57	IDITY	66		
ILT	57	IDLE	66, 67	O	72, 73, 74
IM	57	IER	67	OACH	74
IME	57	IETY	67	OAD	75
IMP	57, 58	IFTER	67	OAK	76, 77
IN	58	IGGER	67	OAL	77, 78
INCH	58	IGGLE	67	OAM	78
IND	58	ILDER	67	OAN	90
INE	58, 59	ILITY	67, 68	OAR	84, 85
ING	59	ILLER	68	OAST	86
INGE	59	ILLION	68	OAT	87
INK	59	ILLY	68	OB	74
INT	59, 60	IMBLE	68	OBE	74
IP	60	IMMER	68	OCK	74, 75
IPE	60	IMPLE	68	OD	75
IR	102	INDER	68	ODE	75
IRCH	102	INDLE	69	OFT	75
IRD	102	INER	69	OG	75, 76

OIL	76	OUNCE	88	OSURE	95
OIN	76	OUND	88	OSY	95
OINT	76	OUNT	88	OTHER	111
OISE	76	OUR	88, 89	OTIC	95, 96
OIST	76	OUSE	89	OTION	96
OKE	76, 77	OUT	89	OTTER	96
OLD	77	OUZ	89	OTTLE	96
OLE	77, 78	OVE	89, 106	OUNDER	96
OLT	78	OW	90	OVER	96, 112
OLVE	78	OWL	90	OWEL	96
OME	78	OWN	90	OWER	96, 97
ON	78	OX	90, 91		
OND	79	OY	91		
ONG	79	OZE	91	U	97
ONT	101	OBBLE	91	UB	97
OO	79, 80	OBBY	91	UCE	82
OOD	80	OCKER	91, 92	UCH	106
OOK	99	ODDER	92	UCT	97
OOL	80	ODDLE	92	UD	97, 98
OOM	81	ODGER	92	UDE	98
OON	81	OGGLE	92	UDGE	98
OOP	81, 82	OILER	92	UFF	98
OOR	82	OKEN	92	UG	98, 99
OOSE	82	OKER	92	UILT	57
OOT	82	OLDEN	92	UK	99
OOTH	82, 83	OLDER	92	UKE	99
OOVE	83	OLER	92, 93	ULE	99
OOZE	83	OLLER	93	ULL	99
OP	83	OLLOW	93	ULSE	99
OPE	83, 84	OLLY	93	ULT	99, 100
ORD	84	OLOGY	93	UM	100
ORE	84, 85	ONIC	93	UME	100
ORM	85	OOMER	94	UMP	100
ORN	85	OONER	94	UN	100
ORSE	85	OOPER	94	UNCH	100
ORT	85, 86	OOTER	94	UND	100, 101
OSE	86	OPIC	94	UNE	101
OSS	86	OPPER	94	UNG	101
OST	86	OPPY	94	UNK	101
OT	86, 87	ORITY	94	UNT	101
OTCH	87	ORMER	94	UP	101
OTE	87	ORROW	94	UPT	101, 102
OTH	87	ORY	95	UR	102
OUD	88	OSION	95	URB	102
OUGH	98	OSIS	95	URCH	102
OUGHT	88	OSITY	95	URD	102
OUL	90	OSTER	95	URE	102, 103

URGE	103	UBBER	107	UNKER	110
URK	103	UBBLE	107	UNNER	110
URL	103	UCKLE	107, 108	UNNY	110
URM	103	UCTION	108	UPPER	110
URN	103, 104	UCTOR	108	URITY	110
URSE	104	UDDER	108	URKY	110
URST	104	UDDLE	108	URNAL	110
URT	104, 105	UDDY	108	URRY	110
URTH	105	UFFER	108	URSION	110
URVE	105	UFFLE	108	USHER	110
US	105	UGGLE	108	USION	110, 111
USH	105	ULSION	108	USTER	111
USK	105	UMBER	108, 109	USTLE	111
UST	105	UMBLE	109	USTY	111
UT	105, 106	UMEN	109	UTER	111
UTCH	106	UMMER	109	UTHER	111
UTE	106	UMMY	109	UTION	111
UTH	82, 83	UMPER	109	UTTER	111, 112
UV	106	UMPTION	109	UTTLE	112
UX	106	UNCTION	109	UVER	112
UZ	106, 107	UNDER	109